ACADEMIC *Listening* ENCOUNTERS

THE NATURAL WORLD

Listening
Note Taking
Discussion

Yoneko

Kanaoka

Low Intermediate

CAMBRIDGE
UNIVERSITY PRESS

CAMBRIDGE UNIVERSITY PRESS
Cambridge, New York, Melbourne, Madrid, Cape Town, Singapore, São Paulo, Delhi

Cambridge University Press
32 Avenue of the Americas, New York, NY 10013-2473, USA

www.cambridge.org
Information on this title: www.cambridge.org/9780521716413

First published 2009

Printed in the United States of America

A catalog record for this book is available from the British Library

ISBN 978-0-521-71639-0 Student's Book
ISBN 978-0-521-71641-3 Teacher's Manual
ISBN 978-0-521-71640-6 Class Audio

Cambridge University Press has no responsibility for the persistence or accuracy of
URLs for external or third-party Internet Web sites referred to in this publication,
and does not guarantee that any content on such Web sites is, or will remain, accurate
or appropriate. Information regarding prices, travel timetables and other factual
information given in this work are correct at the time of first printing but Cambridge
University Press does not guarantee the accuracy of such information thereafter.

It is normally necessary for written permission for copying to be obtained in advance
from a publisher. The tests at the back of this book are designed to be copied and
distributed in class. The normal requirements are waived here and it is not necessary to
write to Cambridge University Press for permission for an individual teacher to make
copies for use within his or her own classroom. Only those pages which carry the
wording '© Cambridge University Press' may be copied.

Cover and book design: Adventure House, NYC
Layout services: Page Designs International, Inc., Fort Lauderdale, Florida

ACADEMIC ENCOUNTERS

The *Academic Encounters* series uses a sustained content approach to teach students the skills they need to be successful in academic courses. There are two books in the series for each content focus: an *Academic Encounters* title and an *Academic Listening Encounters* title. Please consult your catalog or contact your local sales representative for a current list of available titles.

Titles in the *Academic Encounters* series at publication:

Content Focus and Level	Components	*Academic Encounters*	*Academic Listening Encounters*
HUMAN BEHAVIOR High Intermediate to Low Advanced	Student's Book Teacher's Manual Class Audio Cassettes Class Audio CDs	ISBN 978-0-521-47658-4 ISBN 978-0-521-47660-7	ISBN 978-0-521-60620-2 ISBN 978-0-521-57820-2 ISBN 978-0-521-57819-6 ISBN 978-0-521-78357-6
LIFE IN SOCIETY Intermediate to High Intermediate	Student's Book Teacher's Manual Class Audio Cassettes Class Audio CDs	ISBN 978-0-521-66616-9 ISBN 978-0-521-66613-8	ISBN 978-0-521-75483-5 ISBN 978-0-521-75484-2 ISBN 978-0-521-75485-9 ISBN 978-0-521-75486-6
AMERICAN STUDIES Intermediate	Student's Book Teacher's Manual Class Audio CDs	ISBN 978-0-521-67369-3 ISBN 978-0-521-67370-9	ISBN 978-0-521-68432-3 ISBN 978-0-521-68434-7 ISBN 978-0-521-68433-0
THE NATURAL WORLD Low Intermediate	Student's Book Teacher's Manual Class Audio CDs	ISBN 978-0-521-71516-4 ISBN 978-0-521-71517-1	ISBN 978-0-521-71639-0 ISBN 978-0-521-71641-3 ISBN 978-0-521-71640-6

2-Book Sets are available at a discounted price. Each set includes one copy of the Student's Reading Book and one copy of the Student's Listening Book.

Academic Encounters:
Human Behavior 2-Book Set
ISBN 978-0-521-89165-3

Academic Encounters:
American Studies 2-Book Set
ISBN 978-0-521-71013-8

Academic Encounters:
Life in Society 2-Book Set
ISBN 978-0-521-54670-6

Academic Encounters:
The Natural World 2-Book Set
ISBN 978-0-521-72709-9

Contents

Introduction

This Teacher's Manual provides:

- an overview of *Academic Listening Encounters: The Natural World* (page vi)
- a brief description of the *Academic Encounters* series (page vii)
- an overview of *Academic Listening Encounters* Listening, Note Taking, and Discussion books (page vii)
- general teaching guidelines for *Academic Listening Encounters: The Natural World* (page xii)
- answers for the tasks in *Academic Listening Encounters: The Natural World* and additional teaching ideas for each unit (page 1)
- the listening script for *Academic Listening Encounters: The Natural World* (page 59)
- photocopiable lecture quizzes and quiz answers for *Academic Listening Encounters: The Natural World* (page 72)

ABOUT *ACADEMIC LISTENING ENCOUNTERS: THE NATURAL WORLD*

Academic Listening Encounters: The Natural World is a listening, note-taking, and discussion text based on content taught in Earth science and biology courses in high schools, colleges, and universities in the United States.

New Feature in *Academic Listening Encounters: The Natural World*

If you are already familiar with the *Academic Encounters* series, you will discover a new feature in *Academic Listening Encounters: The Natural World*:

- **More support for low-intermediate students**
  The Student's Book is one chapter shorter than previous listening, note-taking, and discussion books in the series, having nine chapters rather than ten. This organization allows more space for tasks that support low-intermediate students in accessing the content of the activities, interviews, and lectures.

Correlation with Standards

Academic Listening Encounters: The Natural World introduces students to topics and skills recognized in the United States secondary school standards for Earth science and biology. For more information about the standards, go to www.cambridge.org/us/esl/academicencounters.

TOEFL® iBT Skills

Like the other *Academic Listening Encounters* books, *Academic Listening Encounters: The Natural World* provides tasks that teach academic skills tested on the TOEFL® iBT test. For a complete list of the tasks, see the Task Index on page 161 of the Student's Book.

THE *ACADEMIC ENCOUNTERS* SERIES

This content-based series is for students who need to improve their academic skills for further study. The series consists of *Academic Encounters* books that help students improve their reading, study skills, and writing; and *Academic Listening Encounters* books that concentrate on listening, note-taking, and discussion skills. The reading and listening books are published as pairs, and each pair focuses on a subject commonly taught in academic courses:

- Topics in Earth science and biology
  Academic Encounters: The Natural World
  Academic Listening Encounters: The Natural World
- Topics in American history and culture
  Academic Encounters: American Studies
  Academic Listening Encounters: American Studies
- Topics in sociology
  Academic Encounters: Life in Society
  Academic Listening Encounters: Life in Society
- Topics in psychology and human communications
  Academic Encounters: Human Behavior
  Academic Listening Encounters: Human Behavior

A reading book and a listening book with the same content focus may be used independently, or they may be used together to teach a complete four-skills course in English for Academic Purposes.

ACADEMIC LISTENING ENCOUNTERS LISTENING, NOTE TAKING, AND DISCUSSION BOOKS

The approach

Focusing on a particular academic discipline allows students to gain a sustained experience with one field and encounter concepts and terminology that overlap and grow more complex. It provides students with a realistic sense of taking an academic course. As language and concepts recur and as their skills develop, students gain confidence in their ability to participate in academic pursuits.

The format

Academic Listening Encounters: Human Behavior, *Academic Listening Encounters: Life in Society*, and *Academic Listening Encounters: American Studies* each consist of five units on different topics within their discipline. *Academic Listening Encounters: The Natural World* consists of four units on different topics within its discipline. In the first three books (*Human Behavior*, *Life in Society*, and *American Studies*), units are divided into two chapters, for a total of ten chapters in each book. In *The Natural World*, the first three units contain two chapters each and the fourth unit contains three chapters, for a total of nine chapters. This organization of *Academic Listening Encounters: The Natural World* allows more space for tasks that support low-intermediate students in accessing the content of the activities, interviews, and lectures that constitute the listening material.

In all books, each chapter has four sections and includes an introductory listening exercise, a selection of informal interviews, an opportunity for students to work on and present a topic-related project, and a two-part academic lecture. A variety of listening, note-taking, and discussion tasks accompany the listening material. Chapters are structured to maximize students' comprehension of the chapter topic. Vocabulary and ideas are recycled through the four sections of each chapter and recur in later chapters, as students move from listening to discussion, and from informal to academic discourse.

A chapter-by-chapter Plan of the Book appears in the front of the Student's Book and an alphabetized Task Index is at the back of the Student's Book.

The audio program

The center of *Academic Listening Encounters* books is their authentic listening material. The Audio Program for each chapter includes a warm-up listening exercise designed to introduce the topic, informal interviews that explore a particular aspect of the chapter topic, and a two-part academic lecture on another aspect of the topic. Each of these three types of listening experience exposes students to a different style of discourse, while recycling vocabulary and concepts.

Tasks that are designed to practice a listening skill and involve listening to the audio material (for example, *Listening for Specific Information*, *Listening for Opinions*, or *Note Taking: Listening for Cause and Effect*), have an earphones icon ⌒ next to the title. This symbol indicates that there is material in the audio program related to the task. A second symbol ▶ PLAY indicates the exact point within the task when the audio material should be played. The complete Audio Program, which contains the recorded material for the listening and note-taking tasks, is available on audio CDs. The listening script of the complete Audio Program is in the third section of this Teacher's Manual. An audio CD of the academic lectures, which are an important part of the Audio Program, is included in the back of each Student's Book to provide students with additional listening practice.

The skills

The three main skills developed in *Academic Listening Encounters* books are listening, note taking, and discussion. Listening is a critical area because unlike text on a page, spoken words are difficult to review. In addition to the content and vocabulary of what they hear, students are challenged by different accents, speeds of delivery, and other features of oral discourse. Tasks in the *Academic Listening Encounters* books guide students in techniques for improving their listening comprehension. These tasks also develop note-taking skills in a structured format that teaches students to write down what they hear in ways that will make it easier to retrieve the information. After the listening and note-taking practice comes an invitation to discussion. Students discuss what they have heard, voice their opinions, compare their experiences, and articulate and exchange viewpoints with other class members, thus making the material their own. Additionally, each chapter gives students the opportunity to work on a project related to the topic, such as conducting a survey or undertaking research, and teaches them the skills necessary to present their findings.

Task commentary boxes

When a task type occurs for the first time in the book, it is usually headed by a colored commentary box that explains what skill is being practiced and why it is important. When the task occurs again later in the book, it may be accompanied by another commentary box, either as a reminder or to present new information about the skill. At the back of the book, there is an alphabetized index of all the tasks. Page references in boldface indicate tasks that are headed by commentary boxes.

Opportunities for student interaction

Many of the tasks in *Academic Listening Encounters* are divided into steps. Some of these steps are to be done by the student working alone, others by students in pairs or in small groups, and still others by the teacher with the whole class. To make the book as lively as possible, student interaction has been built into most activities. Thus, although the books focus on listening and note-taking skills, discussion is fundamental to each chapter. Students often work collaboratively and frequently compare answers in pairs or small groups.

Order of units

The units do not have to be taught in the order in which they appear in the book, although this order is recommended. To a certain extent, tasks do increase in complexity so that, for example, a note-taking task later in the book may draw upon information that has been included in an earlier unit. Teachers who want to use the material out of order may, however, consult the Plan of the Book at the front of the book or the Task Index at the back of the book to see what information has been presented in earlier units.

Course length

Each chapter of a listening, note-taking, and discussion book is divided into four sections and represents approximately 8–18 hours of classroom material, depending on the level of the students. The course can be made shorter or longer – teachers may choose not to do every task in the book and to assign some tasks and listening material for homework rather than do them in class. To lengthen the course, teachers may choose to invite guest speakers, organize debates, and show movies and other authentic recorded material (see Additional Ideas at the end of each unit in this manual).

CHAPTER FORMAT

1 Getting Started

This section contains a short reading task and a listening task. The reading is designed to activate students' prior knowledge about the topic, provide them with general concepts and vocabulary, and stimulate their interest. Comprehension and discussion questions elicit their engagement in the topic.

The listening task in this section is determined by the chapter content and involves one of a variety of responses. The task may require students to complete a chart, do a matching exercise, or listen for specific information. The task provides skill-building practice and also gives students listening warm-up on the chapter topic.

2 American Voices

This section contains informal recorded interviews on issues related to the chapter. It is divided into three subsections:

Before the Interviews

This subsection contains a prelistening task that calls on students to predict the content of the interview or share what they already know about the topic from their personal experience. Take enough time with this task for all students to contribute. The more they invest in the topic at this point, the more they will get out of the interviews.

Interviews

In this subsection, students listen to interviews related to the topic of the chapter. In most chapters the interviewees are native speakers of English, but voices of immigrants to the United States also enrich the discussions. The interviewees are of different ages and ethnic and social backgrounds, allowing students to gain exposure to the rich and diverse reality of speakers of English. The interviews are divided into two parts to facilitate comprehension: each part can include from one to three interviewees.

Each interview segment begins with a boxed vocabulary preview that glosses words and phrases students may not know. The vocabulary is given in the context in which students will hear it. Reading this vocabulary aloud and exploring its meaning within the context will facilitate students' comprehension.

After each vocabulary preview, students are given the opportunity to scan the upcoming task. Then they listen to the interview and go on to complete the particular task, which might include listening for main ideas or details, drawing inferences, or taking notes on the material in order to retell what they have heard. This approach provides a framework for listening, teaches basic listening skills, and allows students to demonstrate their understanding of the interviews.

After the Interviews

In this subsection, students explore the topic more deeply through examining graphic material related to the content of the interviews, thinking critically about what they have heard, or sharing their perspective. Most of the tasks in this section are for pairs or small groups and allow for informal feedback from every student.

3 In Your Own Voice

This section continues to build on the chapter topic and is designed to give students the opportunity to take creative control of the topic at hand. Specific tasks are determined by the chapter content. They may include:

- *Personalizing the content*, in which students talk with partners or in small groups, sharing their experiences and supporting their points of view
- *Gathering data*, in which students conduct surveys or interviews of classmates or people outside the class, or in which they undertake small research projects
- *Presenting data*, in which students organize their data and present it individually or in small groups
- *Responding to presentations*, in which students discuss the content of presentations and analyze the effectiveness of a presenter's style

4 Academic Listening and Note Taking

This section contains a formal, academic lecture related to the topic of the chapter. It is divided into three subsections:

Before the Lecture

The first task of this subsection asks students to predict the content of the lecture, explore what they already know about the topic, or build their background knowledge and vocabulary by doing a task related to a brief reading, syllabus, or other written entry. As with *Before the Interviews*, this section promotes the student's investment in the topic.

Each chapter then proceeds to an academic note-taking skill, determined by the language of the lecture itself and sequenced to build upon skills studied in previous chapters. The skill is explained in a task commentary box, and the listening task is designed to practice it. The recorded material used for the task is drawn from the lecture.

Lecture

In this subsection, students hear the lecture itself. To facilitate comprehension, all lectures are divided into two parts.

Each lecture part begins with a matching or multiple-choice vocabulary task to prepare students for the language they will encounter in the lecture and help them develop their ability to guess meaning from context. Potentially unfamiliar words and phrases are given in the context in which they will be used in the lecture. Reading the items aloud, studying their pronunciation, and exploring their use and meaning will prepare students for hearing them in the lecture.

Following the vocabulary task, students preview a comprehension task designed to provide a framework for their listening and note taking. The task may involve completing a summary or outline, or answering comprehension questions. The task may recycle the note-taking skill taught before the lecture or add a related skill. Students are instructed to take notes during each part of the lecture and then use their notes to complete the lecture comprehension task. Previewing the task will enable students to answer the questions in a more confident and focused manner.

After the Lecture

This subsection invites students to share their perspective through discussion questions that allow them to analyze the chapter content more critically. It may also present additional information or ask students to apply what they have learned.

GENERAL TEACHING GUIDELINES FOR *ACADEMIC LISTENING ENCOUNTERS: THE NATURAL WORLD*

Section Introductions

Each chapter in the Student's Book is divided into four sections. Each section begins with a brief preview: *In this section you will . . .* Always read these previews together with the class and answer any questions that arise. Take enough time with this task for all students to contribute.

Tasks and Commentary Boxes

Virtually every activity throughout *Academic Listening Encounters* books is presented as a task. Each task practices a specific language or thinking skill critical for academic-bound students. Most tasks are recycled throughout the book. (See the Plan of the Book in the front of the Student's Book or the Task Index at the back of the Student's Book.) The first time a task title appears, it is usually followed by a shaded task commentary box containing information about the task. Always read this commentary and check for understanding. Ask students: *What are we doing in this exercise? Why is this useful?*

Listening Tasks

Before students listen to the recorded material and complete the task, make sure that they read over the task and think about what information they will need to listen for.

Replay audio excerpts as many times as you think will benefit the majority of students and enable them to complete tasks successfully. Students are not expected to catch every word; it is not necessary.

As an alternative to the recording, you may try reading the lectures to your students. (See the section titled Listening Script in this Teacher's Manual.) Try to incorporate appropriate stress, intonation, and body language.

In Your Own Voice

In Your Own Voice (Section 3 of each chapter in the Student's Book) usually concludes with students giving oral presentations about a project they have completed. Keep students on task by having them respond to the presentations. They can take notes, ask questions, make comments, and suggest possible ways presenters could improve their style. You may also want to give a content quiz on the presentations. One way to do this is to use your own notes to write one general question about each presentation. Then dictate your questions and allow students to refer to their notes in order to respond.

Photos, Cartoons, and Drawings

All of the art in the Student's Book is intended to build interest and comprehension. In many cases, students are directed to think about the art as part of a task. In cases where they are not specifically asked to do this – such as the art at the beginning of units and chapters – be sure to draw their attention to the art and discuss its connection to the topic.

Vocabulary

Unfamiliar vocabulary is a stumbling block to comprehension, so a great effort has been made to gloss or preteach most of the language that is unfamiliar to students. In each part of Section 2 (American Voices), have students read the vocabulary and glosses in the box by themselves first; then read the vocabulary items aloud so that students can hear how the words are pronounced. Check for understanding of glosses given in the vocabulary boxes.

Each part of the lecture in Section 4 (Academic Listening and Note Taking) begins with a task called Guessing Vocabulary from Context. Begin by reading the vocabulary aloud. When checking the vocabulary task, give the correct answers yourself only as a last resort.

Any photos or realia that you can bring to class will help with comprehension and retention of vocabulary.

Comprehension and Discussion Questions

One of the goals of *Academic Listening Encounters* books is to develop oral fluency, and for this reason there is a great deal of pair and small group work. If students have communicated successfully in pairs or small groups, they will feel more confident about sharing with the class. Let students control the all-class comprehension checks or discussions whenever possible. They can divide up the questions, assigning each one to a different student or pair of students working together. Use the board, and ask for a student volunteer to do the writing. For opinion questions, stress that there are no right or wrong answers. Encourage students to give their own ideas, and model acceptance of all opinions. For comprehension questions – as with vocabulary – give the answers yourself only as a last resort.

Give students plenty of time for discussion questions; circulate and encourage all students to voice their opinions. Whenever possible, pair and group students from different cultures. Move on to the next activity before discussion begins to die out or digress from the subject at hand.

Teacher's Role

As much as you can, try to take part as an equal in discussions and activities. Because many of the tasks in *Academic Listening Encounters* books are based on students' own knowledge and opinions, you should spend most of your time in the role of a participant or facilitator rather than authority figure. You will probably discover that the students are teaching you as much as you are teaching them.

Homework

Some of the activities in *Academic Listening Encounters* books can be done at home. For example, students can read and then think or write about given discussion questions, and they can do the Guessing Vocabulary from Context task before the lecture. They can also do many of the After the Lecture tasks at home, using the notes they took while listening to the lecture. Interviews, research, and surveys are normally done outside of class time.

Encourage students to gain additional listening practice by listening at home to the chapter lectures that are on the audio CD in the back of the Student's Book. Depending on the level of the class, you may want students to listen either before or after you have played the lecture for them in class.

Testing

The lecture in each chapter may be used as a listening and note-taking test. Quizzes on the content of the lectures are in the Lecture Quizzes section of this manual and may be photocopied for distribution to the students. Students may answer each quiz either on the quiz sheet or on their own paper. When taking the tests, students should refer only to the notes they took for the lecture tasks. Answers to the quizzes are in the last section of this manual, Lecture Quiz Answers.

Chapter-by-Chapter Teaching Suggestions and Answer Key

Planet Earth

Unit title page (Student's Book page 1)

Look at the four photographs and have students describe what they see in each picture. Ask students to speculate where each picture was taken and then give their opinions about each location: for example, whether it looks like a good place to live or visit. Point out how diverse Earth is in terms of its natural environments.

Read the unit summary paragraph with students. Introduce them to some of the key words that will be used in the unit: *unique*, *natural features*, *physical structure*, and *landforms*. Chapter 1 discusses Earth's physical structure and some of its famous landforms. Chapter 2 is about plate tectonics and what occurs when the Earth's surface moves: earthquakes and volcanoes.

Because this is the first unit in the book, review the structure of the chapters. Explain that in each chapter students will learn new information and practice their listening skills by listening to interviews and a lecture. Other tasks will help them to refine their note-taking skills. There are many opportunities to discuss the topics of the chapter with classmates. In section 3, In Your Own Voice, students will participate in an individual, group, or class project related to the chapter topic.

Chapter 1

The Physical Earth

1 **GETTING STARTED** (Student's Book pages 2–3)

READING AND THINKING ABOUT THE TOPIC

Answers to step 2 (Student's Book page 3)

1 The four terrestrial planets are Mercury, Venus, Earth, and Mars. The four gas giants are Jupiter, Saturn, Uranus, and Neptune. The difference is that terrestrial planets are made mostly of rock. The gas giants are made mostly of gas.

2 Earth is the only planet in the solar system with liquid water on its surface.

🎧 **LISTENING TO DIRECTIONS**

Answer to step 2 (Student's Book page 3)

Students' drawings should look similar to this diagram:

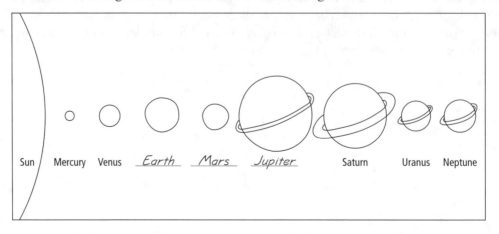

Sun | Mercury | Venus | *Earth* | *Mars* | *Jupiter* | Saturn | Uranus | Neptune

BEFORE THE INTERVIEWS

BUILDING VOCABULARY: UNDERSTANDING WORD PARTS

Answers (Student's Book page 4)

1 geology = the study of the Earth

2 meteorology = the study of the atmosphere
biology = the study of life and living things
seismology = the study of earthquakes
volcanology = the study of volcanoes
hydrology = the study of water

3 geologist = A person who studies the Earth

4 meteorologist = A person who studies the Earth's atmosphere
volcanologist = A person who studies volcanoes
biologist = A person who studies life on Earth
hydrologist = A person who studies water
seismologist = A person who studies earthquakes

SHARING YOUR KNOWLEDGE

Answers to step 1 (Student's Book page 5)

1 seven, five   **4** the Dead Sea
2 Asia, Australia   **5** the Nile
3 Mt. Everest   **6** the Sahara

Answers to step 3 will vary.

INTERVIEW WITH BRAD: Geology

🎧 LISTENING FOR MAIN IDEAS IN AN INTERVIEW

Answers to step 2 (Student's Book page 6)

☑ The meaning of *geology*
☑ The reason Brad decided to become a geologist
☐ The disadvantages of being a geologist
☑ The project Brad is working on now
☐ Brad's future goals
☑ Brad's feelings about geology

Answers to step 3 (Student's Book page 6)

Geologists study what the Earth is made of and how it moves.

From a young age, Brad asked many questions about the Earth: What causes mountains and earthquakes? How do beaches get their shape? and Why do beaches change with the seasons?

At his job right now, Brad is doing research about the shapes of beaches and how each beach changes from season to season and from year to year.

Brad thinks that geology is fun, important, and exciting.

INTERVIEW WITH GABY AND JANE: Earth's natural beauty

🎧 **LISTENING FOR DETAILS**

Answers to step 2 (Student's Book page 8)

Main ideas	Details	
	Grand Canyon	**Uluru (Ayers Rock)**
What it looks like	big – seems to go on forever cliffs go down into earth	*large red rock, middle of plain* *far away looks smooth* *up close rough + has holes*
Its colors	*red, blue, purple, orange, yellow,* *brown*	reddish-brown can change depending on time to pink, purple, or gray
The speakers' thoughts and feelings	one of the most beautiful things ever seen lucky to experience it humans cannot create this	*thinks it's beautiful*
How it was formed	*water flowing over rock*	layers of rock lifted up from Earth softer rocks eroded – Uluru is what's left

Answers to step 3 will vary.

AFTER THE INTERVIEWS

CONSIDERING RELATED INFORMATION (Student's Book page 9)

Students' answers will vary.

3 IN YOUR OWN VOICE (Student's Book page 10)

CONDUCTING RESEARCH

A sample student presentation

I'd like to tell you about the Grand Canyon, a famous natural landmark in the United States. The Grand Canyon is very big. It is almost 450 kilometers long, 24 kilometers wide, and more than 1.6 kilometers deep at its deepest point. It was formed more than 6 million years ago by the Colorado River. The river cut through the land to form the canyon. A lot of rain and ice also wore away the earth and made the canyon bigger. This process is called *erosion* and took millions of years.

The Grand Canyon is famous for many reasons. First, it is famous for its great size. Second, it is famous for its beautiful scenery. Finally, it is famous because geologists can study the layers of the Earth in the walls of the Grand Canyon. For all of these reasons, millions of people visit the Grand Canyon every year.

4 ACADEMIC LISTENING AND NOTE TAKING: The Internal Structure of Earth (Student's Book pages 11–17)

BEFORE THE LECTURE

🎧 LISTENING FOR MAIN IDEAS IN A LECTURE

Answers to step 1 (Student's Book page 11)

2, 1, 4, T, 3

NOTE TAKING: ORGANIZING YOUR NOTES IN AN OUTLINE

Answers to step 1 (Student's Book page 12)

> The Internal Structure of Earth   (lecture topic)
>
> I.   Background information   (main idea)
> II. Crust = Earth's surface layer   (main idea)
>   A. oceanic   (subtopic)
>   B. continental   (subtopic)
> III. Mantle = next layer down from crust   (main idea)
> IV. Core = center of Earth   (main idea)
>   A. outer core   (subtopic)
>   B. inner core   (subtopic)

Answers to step 2 (Student's Book page 12)

There are four main ideas in the lecture. Two main ideas have subtopics.

LECTURE, PART ONE: Background Information About Our Planet

GUESSING VOCABULARY FROM CONTEXT

Answers to step 2 (Student's Book page 13)

1 b, **2** f, **3** h, **4** c, **5** a, **6** e, **7** g, **8** d

🎧 NOTE TAKING: LISTENING FOR SUPPORTING DETAILS

Answers to step 3 (Student's Book page 14)

> The Internal Structure of Earth
>
> I.   Background information
>   4.6 billion years old
>   3rd planet from sun
>   5th largest planet in solar system
>   only planet with liquid water – 71% of surface is covered
>   distance from north pole to south pole = about 13,000 kilometers
>   densest planet
>   Earth's 3 main layers: crust, mantle, core
>   seismic waves (vibrations) give information about Earth's layers

LECTURE, PART TWO: Earth's Internal Structure

GUESSING VOCABULARY FROM CONTEXT

Answers to step 2 (Student's Book page 15)
1 f, **2** e, **3** d, **4** c, **5** a, **6** b

🎧 NOTE TAKING: LISTENING FOR SUPPORTING DETAILS

Sample answers to step 2 (Student's Book page 16)

II. Crust = Earth's surface layer
    A. oceanic
       under water
       6–11 kilometers thick
    B. continental
       land areas
       thicker than oceanic crust (30–40 kilometers)
       movement causes earthquakes, mountains, valleys

III. Mantle = next layer down from crust
    much thicker than crust (2,900 kilometers deep)
    much denser than crust
    most of Earth's mass
    upper – cool, solid rock
    lower – hot and soft

IV. Core = center of Earth
    thicker than the mantle
    A. outer core
       extremely hot – rocks and minerals melt
    B. inner core
       ball of high-pressure material
       solid iron and nickel
       temperatures up to 4,000°C

NOTE TAKING: CLARIFYING YOUR NOTES WITH A PARTNER

(Student's Book page 16)

Students' answers will vary.

USING YOUR NOTES TO LABEL AN ILLUSTRATION

Answers to step 1 (Student's Book page 17)

Students should label the illustration as follows:

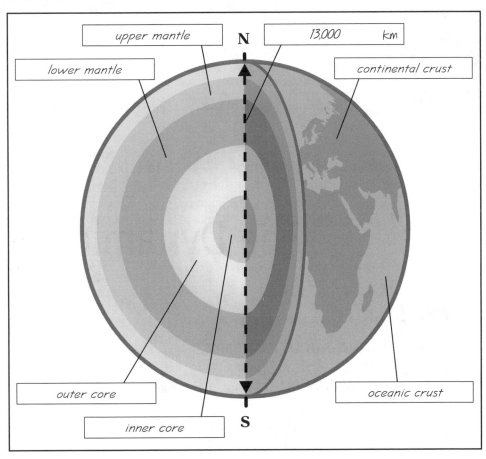

Chapter 1 Lecture Quiz

See the Lecture Quiz section at the back of this Teacher's Manual for a photocopiable quiz on the lecture for Chapter 1. Quiz answers can be found on page 113.

Chapter 2

The Dynamic Earth

1 GETTING STARTED (Student's Book pages 18–20)

READING AND THINKING ABOUT THE TOPIC

Answers to step 2 (Student's Book page 19)

1 Earth's crust is thin, made of hard rock, and broken into many pieces called *plates*.

2 Earth's plates can move away from each other, crash into each other; or slide against each other side by side.

3 Some effects of plate tectonics are volcanoes, earthquakes, and the formation of mountains and valleys.

⌒ LISTENING FOR NUMERICAL INFORMATION ABOUT DISTANCES AND RATES

Answers to step 2 (Student's Book page 19)

1 2.5 cm	**2** 5 mm	**3** 5 cm	**4** 7 cm

Answers to step 3 (Student's Book page 20)

1 40,000 years

2 8,850 meters

3 11.2 million years

4 about 14,286 years

2 AMERICAN VOICES: Loren, Zack, Yoshiko, and Kei

(Student's Book pages 21–25)

BEFORE THE INTERVIEWS

EXAMINING A MAP

Answers (Student's Book page 21)

1 Students' answers will vary.

2 Australia

3 Most volcanoes and earthquakes happen at the edges of the major plates. Tectonic activity happens when the plates push against each other, slide past each other, or move away from each other.

INTERVIEW WITH LOREN: *Living near an active volcano*

ANSWERING MULTIPLE CHOICE QUESTIONS

Answers to step 2 (Student's Book page 22)
1 b, **2** c, **3** a, **4** c, **5** a

Answers to step 3 will vary.

INTERVIEW WITH ZACK AND YOSHIKO: *Living with earthquakes*

DRAWING INFERENCES

Answers to step 2 (Student's Book page 23)
1 T, **2** T, **3** NS, **4** T, **5** F

INTERVIEW WITH KEI: *Surviving the Kobe earthquake*

RETELLING WHAT YOU HAVE HEARD

Answers to step 2 (Student's Book page 24)

1 Kei felt a strong shaking movement, first up and down, then side to side. She heard her neighbor screaming.

2 Everything in her apartment fell down. Dishes fell down. The staircase leading to her apartment fell down. The highway and many houses fell down.

3 After the earthquake, they did not have running water in their home for two or three months. They also didn't have gas or electricity for a long time.

4 On the day of the earthquake, Kei didn't feel scared. She was grateful that her home and family weren't hurt. Now, she remembers how she felt during the earthquake, but she still isn't afraid.

Answers to step 3 will vary.

AFTER THE INTERVIEWS

CONSIDERING RELATED INFORMATION (Student's Book page 25)

Students' answers will vary.

THINKING CRITICALLY ABOUT THE TOPIC

Sample answers (Student's Book page 25)

1 No, they are not afraid of earthquakes. They are both prepared for earthquakes, but not afraid.

2 They don't live their lives afraid of what will happen in the future. Kei says we don't know what will happen tomorrow, and Zack says people can't live their lives in fear.

3 Students' answers will vary.

3 IN YOUR OWN VOICE (Student's Book pages 26–27)

CONSIDERING RELATED INFORMATION

Sample answers to step 5 (Student's Book page 27)

Theory of plate tectonics Evidence chart	
Group	**Notes**
Shape of continents	When we look at the shape of today's continents, we can see that they can fit together like puzzle pieces.
Fossils	Scientists have found fossils of the same species of plants and animals on different continents. For example, they have found the same plant in Africa and Antarctica and fossils of the same animal in Africa and Asia. This suggests these continents were once connected.
Animals	The same animals can be found far apart on different continents, for example, marsupials in Australia and North America. These animals can't travel across the ocean, so these continents were probably once connected by land.
Mountains	Mountains start on one continent and seem to continue on another. For example, old mountains on Africa's west coast line up with east coast mountains in South America.
Rocks and minerals	The same kinds of rocks can be found on different continents, for example, diamonds in South Africa and Argentina.

BEFORE THE LECTURE
BUILDING BACKGROUND KNOWLEDGE AND VOCABULARY
Answers to step 2 (Student's Book page 28)

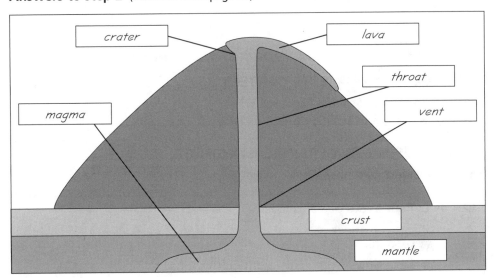

🎧 NOTE TAKING: FOCUSING ON THE INTRODUCTION
Answers to step 1 (Student's Book page 29)
1 Today's lecture is going to be about
2 I'd like to start today's lecture by introducing
3 Then I'll describe
4 Finally, we'll discuss

LECTURE, PART ONE: The Basic Structure of a Volcano
GUESSING VOCABULARY FROM CONTEXT
Answers to step 2 (Student's Book page 30)
1 d, **2** b, **3** a, **4** c

🎧 NOTE TAKING: USING TELEGRAPHIC LANGUAGE
Sample answers to step 1 (Student's Book page 30)
1 ~~Well~~, volcanoes form when molten rock, ~~or~~ magma, makes ~~its~~ way up from ~~the~~ Earth's upper mantle.
2 ~~The~~ upper mantle ~~is about~~ 80 to 150 kilometers below ~~the~~ Earth's surface, ~~where the~~ temperatures ~~are~~ so high ~~that~~ rocks and minerals ~~start to~~ melt.
3 ~~The~~ melting rocks and minerals form magma, ~~and this magma~~ rises up through ~~the solid~~ mantle.

4 ~~Usually an~~ eruption starts because ~~an~~ earthquake breaks ~~the~~ rock ~~at the~~ top of ~~the~~ mantle, ~~and the~~ opening ~~in the rock~~ releases pressure on ~~the~~ gases in ~~the~~ magma.

5 ~~The~~ magma ~~then~~ rises to ~~the~~ surface through ~~a~~ narrow passageway, ~~or what we call the~~ throat ~~of a volcano, and~~ erupts at ~~an~~ opening in ~~the~~ crust, ~~called a~~ vent.

Answers to step 3 (Student's Book page 31)
Part One: Structure of a Volcano
2, 5, 6, 1, 3, 4

LECTURE, PART TWO: Four Types of Volcanoes

GUESSING VOCABULARY FROM CONTEXT

Answers to step 2 (Student's Book page 32)
1 h, **2** d, **3** j, **4** f, **5** b, **6** a, **7** i, **8** c, **9** e, **10** g

⌒ NOTE TAKING: USING TELEGRAPHIC LANGUAGE

Sample answers to step 2 (Student's Book pages 32–33)

Part Two: Four Types of Volcanoes
  I. Shield volcanoes
      A. Very big
      B. Lava flows from vent – gentle eruptions
      C. Lava cools, becomes hard
         forms broad, sloping shape, circular base
      D. Example: Mauna Loa, Big Island, Hawaii
         = largest volcano – starts on sea floor, rises to over 9,000 m high

 II. Composite volcanoes
      A. Smaller – up to 2,500 m
      B. Both explosive and gentle eruptions
         1. Explosive: layers of ash and rock pile up at vent
         2. Gentle: lava flows cover layers of ash, makes alternating layers
      C. Steeper slopes, fewer eruptions
      D. Examples
         1. Mt. Fuji, Japan
         2. Mt. St. Helens

III. Cinder cone volcanoes
      A. Smallest – less than 200 m
      B. Form when lava cools quickly in the air and hardens, breaks
         into cinders
      C. Cinders pile around vent, form cone with bowl-shaped crater
      D. Form 100s to 1,000s of cones
      E. Example: Paricutín, Mexico
         1. 1943
         2. Grew to 340 m in a few months

IV. Supervolcanoes
   A. Biggest volcanoes, most <u>explosive</u> eruptions
   B. Don't form <u>cones</u> – leave <u>huge</u> <u>crater in ground</u>
   C. Rare but can cause <u>widespread destruction</u>
   D. Example: Toba
      1. <u>70,000–75,000</u> years ago in Indonesia
      2. Killed <u>60 percent of people</u> on Earth
V. Warning signs before an eruption
   A. <u>Earthquakes</u>
   B. Ground cracks
   C. Drinking water <u>tastes different</u>, may mean change in groundwater
   D. Glaciers <u>on top of volcanoes melt</u>

AFTER THE LECTURE

USING YOUR NOTES TO MAKE A STUDY SHEET

Sample answers (Student's Book page 34)

Volcano types	Key points
	Volcano type: cinder cone • smaller – usually less than 200 m • lava cools quickly, hardens & breaks into small cinders – forms bowl-shaped crater • ex = Paricutín, Mexico
	Volcano type: shield • very big • lava flows gently over surface • broad, sloping shape, circular base • ex = Mauna Loa, Hawaii (9,000 m)
	Volcano type: composite • small – up to 2,500 m • explosive & gentle eruptions – alternating layers of ash & rock form steep cone • ex = Mt. Fuji, Mt. St. Helens
	Volcano type: supervolcano • biggest volcanoes • explosive eruptions leave huge craters, no cone • rare but destructive • largest = Toba – 70,000–75,000 years ago – killed 60 percent people on Earth

Chapter 2 Lecture Quiz

See the Lecture Quiz section at the back of this Teacher's Manual for a photocopiable quiz on the lecture for Chapter 2. Quiz answers can be found on page 113.

Additional Ideas for Unit 1

Key topics in this unit include the solar system, unique features of Earth, Earth's internal structure, plate tectonics, natural landforms, and tectonic activity (earthquakes and volcanoes).

1 Watch a movie in class about space and space travel, the possibility of life on other planets, and / or tectonic events on Earth. Some movies with these themes are *Contact*, *Independence Day*, *Apollo 13*, *The Right Stuff*, *Volcano*, *Dante's Peak*, and *10.5*. Have students discuss how the film relates to this unit, as well as any inaccuracies they find presented in the film.

2 Invite a guest speaker to your class who has traveled to one or more famous natural landmarks in the world. Have him or her describe the physical features of the landmark, as well as any geological information about it (how it was formed, its composition, etc.). If possible, have the speaker share photos of the site.

3 Bring in color photos of several natural landmarks in different countries (some examples: Mt. Everest, Manicouagan Crater, Geiranger Fjord, Monument Valley, Bryce Canyon, Meteor Crater, the Devil's Marbles, Haytor on Dartmoor, Vale of Glamorgan, NaPali Cliffs). Have students describe and discuss the photos, including how they think these landmarks were formed and which ones they would be interested in visiting.

4 Have students research the story of Mt. Paricutín, or another famous volcano or earthquake that occurred in modern or ancient history. Students can then retell the story to a partner or in small groups.

5 Have students research the planets in our solar system in more detail. This could be done in groups, with each group assigned to one planet. Another group could research the sun. Groups can make posters or models of their planet, and describe its internal structure, surface features, atmosphere, and unusual characteristics. Conduct a class discussion about the possibility of life on other planets. Students could also research and discuss their opinion of the decision to remove Pluto from the list of planets in the solar system.

Water on Earth

Unit title page (Student's Book page 35)

Have students look at the unit opener photo to see if they can recognize the structure of a water molecule. You may need to explain that two or more atoms bonded together form a molecule, and that water has a very simple molecular structure: two hydrogen atoms and one oxygen atom. This would be a good time to introduce how to write and say the chemical formula for water, H_2O. You may want to lead a discussion on some of the unique features of water: It has surface tension, it expands and becomes less dense when frozen, it occurs naturally on Earth in all three states (liquid, solid, gas), and it is the most abundant substance on Earth and in the human body.

Read the unit title and ask students what they think they will study in this chapter. As students respond, list their answers on the board and, if possible, group them into two categories: freshwater and saltwater. Explain that in this unit, students will study both. Chapter 3 is about freshwater, and Chapter 4 examines Earth's oceans. Both chapters explore the critical role water plays in the lives of humans on Earth, as well as some of the current threats to our most valuable natural resource. Read the unit summary paragraph with students and explain any new vocabulary words.

Chapter 3

Earth's Water Supply

1 GETTING STARTED (Student's Book pages 36–38)

READING AND THINKING ABOUT THE TOPIC

Answers to step 2 (Student's Book page 37)
1 The total water supply on Earth is exactly the same as it was 4.6 billion years ago.
2 Answers may include: water vapor in the air, clouds, rain, lakes, rivers, oceans, ice, groundwater, water in plants, and water in animals and humans.

BUILDING BACKGROUND KNOWLEDGE (Student's Book page 37)

Answers to steps 1 and 2 will vary.

🎧 PERSONALIZING THE TOPIC

Answers to step 1 (Student's Book page 38)

1 ocean	3 river	5 lake
2 ice	4 waterfall	

Answers to step 2 (Student's Book page 38)

1 lake	3 waterfall	5 river
2 ocean	4 ice	

BEFORE THE INTERVIEWS

EXAMINING GRAPHIC MATERIAL

Answers to step 1 (Student's Book page 39)

1 United States; Ethiopia

2 Answers will vary but may include differences in the countries' population, geography, climate, agricultural practices, industrial development, political conditions, and the lifestyles and daily practices of its people.

3 Students' answers will vary.

Answers to step 2 (Student's Book page 39)

1 c, **2** b, **3** a

INTERVIEW WITH GINA: Water in the United States

🎧 LISTENING FOR OPINIONS

Answers to step 2 (Student's Book page 40)

2, 3, 5, 6

INTERVIEW WITH LARA AND DAVID: Water in Cambodia

🎧 USING A MAP TO UNDERSTAND COMPLEX CONCEPTS

Answers to step 2 (Student's Book page 42)

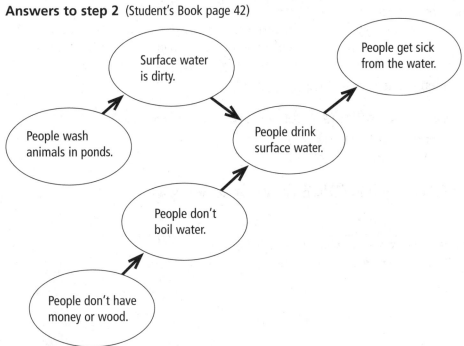

Answer to step 4 (Student's Book page 42)

Lara and David introduced a water filter to help clean the water.

INTERVIEW WITH SEÓNAGH: *Water in Africa*

🎧 **LISTENING FOR SPECIFIC INFORMATION**

Answers to step 1 (Student's Book page 43)

1 Just over a year

2 At first, she boiled her water or bought bottled water. Later, she did the same thing as other people living in Cameroon.

3 Some parts of Cameroon have good roads and easy access to water, but other parts have bad roads and poor access. People living in the disadvantaged areas have to travel very far to get water.

4 People are hardworking and able to survive under difficult conditions. They are also less wasteful of natural resources.

5 She appreciates the easy access to clean water in her home country, and she is more aware of and careful about how much water she uses.

Answers to step 2 (Student's Book page 44)

Water comes from the (sky /(Earth)) and flows across the Earth. It's like ((blood)/ food). In some cultures, water is seen as the ((blood)/ child) of the Earth. I think of it that way. I think of ((the world)/ nature) as being interconnected and all people being interconnected, all (countries /(continents)), and all of our lives. So I think of water as sort of a metaphor for that.

AFTER THE INTERVIEWS

EXAMINING A MAP

Answers (Student's Book page 44)

1 Answers will vary but may include the size of the country's population, its geography and climate, agricultural and industrial practices, infrastructure, economy, political conditions, and the lifestyle and daily practices of its people.

2 Students' answers will vary.

APPLYING WHAT YOU HAVE LEARNED (Student's Book page 45)

Answers to step 1 will vary.

3 IN YOUR OWN VOICE (Student's Book pages 46–47)

PERSONALIZING THE TOPIC

Answers to step 1 (Student's Book page 46)

1 b, 2 d, 3 a, 4 c, 5 e

ACADEMIC LISTENING AND NOTE TAKING: Earth's Freshwater Supply (Student's Book pages 48–55)

BEFORE THE LECTURE

PREDICTING THE CONTENT

Answers to step 1 (Student's Book page 48)
4, 2, 3, 1

Answers to step 2 (Student's Book page 48)
1 c, **2** b, **3** d, **4** a

🎧 NOTE TAKING: USING SYMBOLS AND ABBREVIATIONS

Answers to step 1 (Student's Book page 49)
1 g, **2** a, **3** d, **4** i, **5** b, **6** j, **7** h, **8** e, **9** f, **10** c

Sample answers to step 2 (Student's Book page 49)
1 Most of E's surf covd in H_2O
2 97% = salt H_2O; 3% fr H_2O
3 Of all fresh H_2O: 75% = ice, only 25% = liquid
4 <1% H_2O on E = drinking H_2O for all ppl
5 H_2O on surf of E = surf H_2O; beneath E's surf = ground H_2O

LECTURE, PART ONE: Sources and Functions of Surface Water

GUESSING VOCABULARY FROM CONTEXT

Answers to step 2 (Student's Book page 50)
1 g, **2** b, **3** a, **4** e, **5** h, **6** f, **7** c, **8** d

🎧 NOTE TAKING: USING SYMBOLS AND ABBREVIATIONS

Sample answers to step 1 (Student's Book page 51)

Word	Abbreviation	Word	Abbreviation
ground	grnd	irrigation	irrig
stream	str	environment	envir
river	riv	quality	qual
natural	nat	pollution	poll

Sample answers to step 2 (Student's Book page 51)

I. Where does fresh H_2O come from?
   A. Rain + snow falls → sinks into grnd
     If grnd is full of H_2O, then stays on surf
   B. Small flow of perm water = str
     If combine, become bigger = riv
   C. May form pond/lake, or flow to ocean

II. Functions of fresh H_2O
- A. Rivers carry nutrients + minerals ∴ nearby land rich + fertile
  In drier areas, H_2O carried from <u>nat</u> sources to farm (this proc called <u>irrig</u>)
- B. Daily tasks, ex washing dishes + clothes, cleaning + bathing
- C. Industry
- D. Transportation
- E. Playing + enjoyment
- F. * most <u>imp</u> = clean H_2O for humans + <u>anim</u> to drink
  w/o surf H_2O, life on <u>E</u> could not exist

LECTURE, PART TWO: *Threats to Earth's Freshwater Supply*

GUESSING VOCABULARY FROM CONTEXT

Answers to step 2 (Student's Book page 52)
1 a, **2** h, **3** f, **4** d, **5** c, **6** e, **7** g, **8** b

⌒ NOTE TAKING: USING BULLETS AND BRACKETS TO ORGANIZE YOUR NOTES

Sample answers to step 2 (Student's Book page 53)

2. <u>Poll</u>
   - many sources, ex factories, hum waste, pest + fert ⎫
   - poll in air: <u>acid rain</u>: falls to E, enters H_2O supply ⎬ some H_2O too <u>polluted</u> to use
   - trash enters strm or riv ⎭

3. Overuse by humans
   - H_2O cannot ↑, but pop ↑ every yr ⎫
   - millions more ppl → <u>use + drink H_2O</u> → need for ⎬ WWC: > 1 billion ppl, not enough
     more <u>food</u> → more farming → more <u>H_2O</u> for <u>irrig</u> ⎪ clean, safe H_2O
   - H_2O used by ppl doubling every 20 yrs ⎭

CONCLUSION
   - new tech for <u>irrig</u> → less H_2O wasted ⎫
   - ppl make small changes in daily practs ⎬ Humans must learn to use
   - all countries coop to prev <u>poll</u> + manage H_2O ⎭ H_2O better

AFTER THE LECTURE

REWRITING YOUR NOTES AFTER A LECTURE (Student's Book page 54)
Students' answers will vary.

CONSIDERING RELATED INFORMATION (Student's Book page 55)
Students' answers will vary.

Chapter 3 Lecture Quiz

See the Lecture Quiz section at the back of this Teacher's Manual for a photocopiable quiz on the lecture for Chapter 3. Quiz answers can be found on page 113.

Earth's Oceans

1 **GETTING STARTED** (Student's Book pages 56–57)

READING AND THINKING ABOUT THE TOPIC

Answers to step 2 (Student's Book page 57)

1 Seas, bays, and gulfs are much smaller than oceans and are partly surrounded by land.
2 All bodies of saltwater are connected, and the same water flows from one sea or ocean into the next.
3 Only 5 percent of the world ocean has been explored by scientists; 71 percent of Earth's surface is covered by ocean water; 99 percent of Earth's total livable space is in the ocean.

SHARING YOUR OPINION (Student's Book page 57)

Answers to steps 2 and 3 will vary.

2 **AMERICAN VOICES: Edmund and Tomoki** (Student's Book pages 58–62)

BEFORE THE INTERVIEWS

SHARING YOUR OPINION (Student's Book page 58)

Answers to steps 2–4 will vary.

PREDICTING THE CONTENT

Answers to step 2 (Student's Book page 59)
1 T, 2 E, 3 E, 4 E, 5 T

INTERVIEW WITH EDMUND: *Diving*

🎧 RETELLING WHAT YOU HAVE HEARD

Sample answers to step 3 (Student's Book page 60)

1 When Edmund goes diving, he sometimes finds interesting things in the ocean, like old bottles.

2 One time Edmund saw a seahorse and took a picture of it.

3 Eels have hit Edmund a few times. This was a scary experience for him.

4 One time Edmund saw two whales, a mother and her baby, while he was diving. When the whales heard Edmund, they swam away.

INTERVIEW WITH TOMOKI: *Surfing*

🎧 LISTENING FOR MAIN IDEAS

Answers to step 2 (Student's Book page 61)

1 Why did Tomoki start surfing?

__✓__ He has always been interested in the sport.

__✓__ His friend gave him a surfboard.

_____ His father taught him how to surf.

2 Why does Tomoki love surfing?

__✓__ He loves being in the water.   _____ He loves being in the sun.

__✓__ Surfing is challenging.   _____ Surfing is easy.

__✓__ The ocean is beautiful.   __✓__ Surfing is unique.

3 According to Tomoki, what does a surfer need to surf well?

__✓__ physical fitness   _____ very big waves

__✓__ good balance   _____ strong wind

_____ a good surfboard   __✓__ a clean ocean surface

🎧 THINKING CRITICALLY ABOUT THE TOPIC

Answer to step 1 (Student's Book page 61)

Edmund and Tomoki think that humans (can /(cannot)) control the ocean.

AFTER THE INTERVIEWS

THINKING CREATIVELY ABOUT THE TOPIC

Answers to step 1 (Student's Book page 62)

1 T, 2 E

3 IN YOUR OWN VOICE (Student's Book page 63)

PERSONALIZING THE TOPIC

Answers to steps 1 and 2 will vary.

4 ACADEMIC LISTENING AND NOTE TAKING: Earth's
Oceans (Student's Book pages 64–72)

BEFORE THE LECTURE
BUILDING BACKGROUND KNOWLEDGE

Answers to steps 1 and 2 (Student's Book pages 64–65)

1 The Arctic Ocean is almost completely surrounded by land.

2 The Mariana Trench, the world's deepest place, is located in the Pacific Ocean.

3 The currents in the Indian Ocean change direction during the year, which causes monsoons (strong winds and heavy rains).

4 The Atlantic Ocean is the least salty ocean because many rivers run into it.

5 The Southern Ocean is sometimes called the Antarctic Ocean.

6 The Southern Ocean surrounds the coldest, windiest place on Earth.

7 The Pacific Ocean has more water than all of the other oceans combined.

8 The Atlantic Ocean is slowly growing larger because of plate tectonics.

NOTE TAKING: LISTENING FOR SIGNAL WORDS

Answers to step 1 (Student's Book page 66)

and so on	signaling an incomplete list
as I just said	referring to information mentioned earlier
as you know	referring to background information
consequently	introducing an effect
for example	introducing an example
incidentally	introducing additional information
in fact	emphasizing

Answers to step 3 (Student's Book page 66)

1 and so on   3 As I just said   5 For example   7 In fact
2 As you know   4 Consequently   6 Incidentally

LECTURE, PART ONE: The World Ocean
GUESSING VOCABULARY FROM CONTEXT

Answers to step 2 (Student's Book page 67)
1 f, 2 a, 3 d, 4 c, 5 b, 6 e

NOTE TAKING: USING HANDOUTS TO HELP YOU TAKE NOTES

Students' questions for step 2 will vary. (Student's Book page 68)
In groups or as a class, discuss any parts of the handout that students questioned.

LECTURE, PART TWO: The Layers of the Ocean
GUESSING VOCABULARY FROM CONTEXT

Answers to step 2 (Student's Book page 69)
1 c, 2 i, 3 d, 4 h, 5 j, 6 f, 7 g, 8 a, 9 b, 10 e

Sample answers to step 1 (Student's Book page 70)

avg ocean depth = <u>3,800</u> m
interesting feature = layered structure b/c of diff densities

1) Surface – top <u>100</u> to <u>200</u> m
   Warm H_2O less <u>dense</u> so stays at surface; cold H_2O <u>sinks</u>
   Most fish + marine life live here b/c <u>plants to eat</u>

2) Middle – goes to <u>1,000</u> m
   Rapid drop in temp, from <u>15°C</u> at surface to <u>4°C</u> at 1,000 m
   Little sunlight = no plants, ∴ animals have to <u>swim to surf</u>

3) Bottom – below <u>1,000</u> m
   No sunlight, almost freezing temps
   Animals have spec adaptations, for ex 1. <u>no eyes</u>
                                                   2. give off own light

   Scientists still don't know much

LECTURE, PART THREE: Water Pressure

🎧 **NOTE TAKING: USING HANDOUTS TO HELP YOU TAKE NOTES**

Sample answers to step 1 (Student's Book page 71)

H_2O denser than air ∴ more pressure
• every 10 m ↓ into ocn = +1 atmosphere of pressure
• ocn bottom = press as high as 600 atm (600 kg per cm^2)

Concl 1) 4 main ocns + seas – all interconnected
        2) ocns deep, layered
        3) pressure ↑ w/ depth

Ocn = last unexplored region on E

🎧 **NOTE TAKING: FOCUSING ON THE CONCLUSION** (Student's Book page 72)

Students' answers will vary.

AFTER THE LECTURE

MAKING TEST QUESTIONS FROM YOUR NOTES

Answers to step 1 (Student's Book page 72)

1 The surface layer (sunlit zone), the middle layer, and the bottom layer (midnight zone)

2 Because there is no light here, and therefore it is pitch black

3 Water in the surface layer is relatively warm compared to the bottom layer. The surface layer has an average temperature of 15°C, and the bottom layer has very cold, almost freezing temperatures.

4 At 20 meters deep, the water pressure of the ocean is 3 atmospheres, or 3 kilograms per square centimeter.

Students' answers to step 2 will vary.

Chapter 4 Lecture Quiz

See the Lecture Quiz section at the back of this Teacher's Manual for a photocopiable quiz on the lecture for Chapter 4. Quiz answers can be found on page 113.

Additional Ideas for Unit 2

Key topics in this unit include the hydrologic cycle, water conservation, the importance of maintaining a plentiful supply of freshwater for all people, and access to water in the United States and other countries. The unit also discusses water sports, facts about Earth's five oceans, and features of ocean water.

1 Organize a field trip in which you and your students participate in a stream or beach cleanup (or another local water conservation project). After the project, have students reflect on their experiences in a journal, group discussion, or oral report.

2 Invite a guest speaker from the local water supply board or an environmental organization to the class. Have him/her discuss what water-related challenges the community is facing, what their organization is doing to protect natural water resources, and how students can get involved and help.

3 Have students interview five people outside of class. They should ask each interviewee about their water usage habits and what actions they take to conserve water. Students can share the results of their interviews in class and compile a class list of water conservation tips.

4 Have students reflect on the universal importance of water by discussing proverbs that contain references to water from different countries. Some examples:

We never know the worth of water until the well is dry. (France)
Even hard rocks can be broken by persistent soft drops of water. (Portugal)
Don't spit in the well – you may need to drink from it! (Russia)
Don't empty the water jar until the rain falls. (Philippines)
The frog does not drink up the pond in which he lives. (United States / Native American)
A coconut shell full of water is an ocean to an ant. (India)
When you drink the water, remember the spring. (China)
After a thousand years, water returns to its home. (Mexico)
Any water in the desert will do. (Saudi Arabia)

Students should first discuss what they think each proverb means. Then they can share proverbs containing references to water from their own countries.

5 Conduct a simple experiment in class. Put cold water into a clear glass container. In a separate container, add red food coloring to warm water. Ask students to predict what will happen when you pour the red water into the clear water. Gently add the water and ask students to describe and explain what they see. Finally, ask students how their observations connect to the information they learned in Chapter 4.

6 In groups, have students research current environmental problems related to Earth's oceans and freshwater supply. Some possible topics are the rising sea level, dead zones, depletion of marine life, destruction of coral reefs, and melting of polar ice. Each group should prepare a problem/solution poster about their issue and present it to the class.

7 Have students research the different types of marine life that live in the surface, middle, and bottom layers of the ocean. They can create posters with pictures and interesting facts about their sea animal of choice. If possible, have them draw connections between features of the animal and aspects of the ocean level (temperature, light, pressure, etc.) that they learned about in the Chapter 4 lecture.

8 Bring in several different kinds of drinking water (safe tap water and different brands of bottled water). Have small groups of students conduct their own blind taste test, then compare preferences as a class. Students can discuss what (if any) differences they detect in the different waters. They should also consider the price of the different bottled waters, what information can be found on the bottle's label (for example, phrases like "filtered" and "mountain spring"), and the influence of packaging and advertising.

9 You may want to watch some movies related to this unit with your students. *Erin Brockovich* is based on the true story of a single mother who fights against a power company that pollutes the water supply of a town in California. *An Inconvenient Truth* is an Oscar-winning documentary about global warming that addresses, among other topics, melting polar ice and the rising sea level. *Waterworld* is a science fiction film that takes place in a future world that is entirely covered with water.

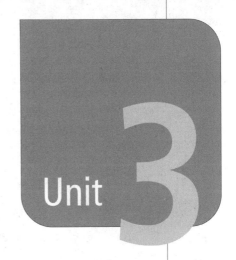

The Air Around Us

Unit title page (Student's Book page 73)

Read the unit title and ask students to describe what is happening in the photo, and what is enabling it to happen. Students will probably answer "wind" or "air." You can then introduce the scientific term for air – *atmosphere* – and explain that the atmosphere is the layer of air that surrounds Earth, from the ground all the way up to where space begins.

Read the summary of Chapter 5. Elicit students' ideas about what kinds of things can be found in the air and what constitutes good air quality versus bad air quality. You may also want to ask if any student has been to a place with poor air quality, and then have that individual explain how the air felt and how it affected him or her. In Chapter 5, students will learn about a number of factors that affect air quality, such as humidity, air pressure, and various kinds of particulate matter.

Read the summary of Chapter 6. Elicit from students all the types of weather they know and list them on the board. Explain the meaning of "severe weather," and then ask students to predict the kinds of weather from the list on the board that they think will be in the chapter (the interviews are about a blizzard, a flood, and a hurricane). You may also want to ask students if any of them have ever experienced severe weather. Finally, ask students what they have heard about global warming. The Chapter 6 lecture explains the difference between the natural and enhanced greenhouse effect, as well as the changes effected by global warming on our planet.

Chapter 5

Earth's Atmosphere

1 GETTING STARTED (Student's Book pages 74–75)

READING AND THINKING ABOUT THE TOPIC

Answers to step 2 (Student's Book page 75)

1 Yes and no. All air on Earth is made of the same gases. However, the quality of air is not the same in all places on Earth.

2 Three factors that affect air quality are: 1) humidity – how much water is in the air; 2) particulates – small pieces of dirt, dust, and other matter in the air; and 3) air pressure – how strongly the air presses around us on Earth's surface.

🎧 LISTENING FOR BACKGROUND NOISE

Answers to step 1 (Student's Book page 75)
Answers will vary, but students should identify the action depicted in each box from left to right: sweating, sneezing, gasping, coughing.

Answers to step 2 (Student's Book page 75)
  _b_   in the countryside   _c_ at the top of a mountain
  _d_   in the city   _a_ in a rain forest

Answers to step 3 (Student's Book page 75)
  _c_   The air is thin.   _b_ There's pollen in the air.
  _a_   It is very humid.   _d_ It's smoggy.

Answers to step 4 (Student's Book page 75)

a This person is in a rain forest and is sweating because it is very humid.

b This person is in the countryside and is sneezing because there's pollen in the air.

c This person is at the top of a mountain and is gasping because the air is thin.

d This person is in the city and is coughing because it's smoggy.

2 AMERICAN VOICES: Jeff, Shari, Kelley, and Michael

(Student's Book pages 76–81)

BEFORE THE INTERVIEWS

BUILDING BACKGROUND KNOWLEDGE AND VOCABULARY

Answers to step 2 (Student's Book page 76)

Natural sources: volcanoes, wildfires, windstorms, trees

Man-made sources: cars, airplanes, factories, wildfires

NOTE: Wildfires can be categorized as either natural or man-made, depending on what starts the wildfire, for example: lightning or volcanic eruption (natural causes), or arson or human carelessness (man-made causes).

EXAMINING A MAP

Answers (Student's Book page 77)

1 There are more dry areas in the world.

2 Africa has the most dry areas.

3 Answers will vary.

4 Answers will vary.

INTERVIEW WITH JEFF: Pollutants in the air

🎧 LISTENING FOR SPECIFIC INFORMATION

Answers to step 2 (Student's Book page 78)

Jeff is the director of an environmental group. He is concerned about <u>air quality</u> and its effects on <u>people</u> and <u>nature</u>. In this interview, Jeff talks about <u>pollutants</u> in the air, from both <u>man-made</u> activity and <u>natural</u> sources.

Answers to step 3 (Student's Book page 78)

cars, windstorms, factories, wildfires

INTERVIEW WITH SHARI: Air quality

🎧 LISTENING FOR SPECIFIC INFORMATION

Answers to step 1 (Student's Book page 79)

3, 1, 5, 4, 2

Answers to step 2 (Student's Book page 79)

If you hear on the news that today's smog level advisory is "4," it means that the air is (clear /(smoggy)) and it is (safe /(dangerous)) to exercise outside.

INTERVIEW WITH KELLEY AND MICHAEL: Humid and dry environments

🎧 ANSWERING MULTIPLE CHOICE QUESTIONS

Answers to step 1 (Student's Book pages 80–81)
1 b, **2** a, **3** a, **4** a, **5** a, **6** b, **7** b, **8** a

AFTER THE INTERVIEWS

SHARING YOUR OPINION (Student's Book page 81)

Students' answers will vary.

3 IN YOUR OWN VOICE (Student's Book pages 82–83)

CONDUCTING AN EXPERIMENT

Experiment results and students' reports will vary.

4 ACADEMIC LISTENING AND NOTE TAKING: What Is in the Air Out There? (Student's Book pages 84–89)

BEFORE THE LECTURE

PREDICTING THE CONTENT

Answers to step 1 (Student's Book page 84)
1 Air is made up of 12 gases.
2 Nitrogen and oxygen
3 Humid
4 Dry or arid
5 Particulate matter/particulates
6 Possible answers include: smoggy, hazy, or polluted
7 Possible answers include: volcanoes, wildfires, windstorms, or trees.
8 Possible answers include: cars, airplanes, factories, or wildfires.
9 Possible answers include: sneezing, coughing, breathing problems, damage to the lungs, headaches, or irritated eyes or throat.

Answer to step 2 (Student's Book page 84)
The most comfortable level for most people is 50 percent humidity.

Answer to step 3 (Student's Book page 84)
The major sources of humidity mentioned in the lecture are precipitation and water vapor from oceans, rivers, trees, plants, and the ground.

🎧 NOTE TAKING: IDENTIFYING KEY VOCABULARY IN THE LECTURE

Answers to step 1 (Student's Book page 85)
1 c, **2** e, **3** b, **4** d, **5** a

Answers to step 2 (Student's Book page 85)

1 b, **2** e, **3** a, **4** c, **5** d

LECTURE, PART ONE: Humidity

GUESSING VOCABULARY FROM CONTEXT

Answers to step 2 (Student's Book page 86)

1 d, **2** c, **3** e, **4** b, **5** a

🎧 NOTE TAKING: ORGANIZING YOUR NOTES IN AN OUTLINE

Sample answers to step 2 (Student's Book page 87)

The Air We Breathe

I. Gases
   A. Nitrogen makes up 78%
   B. Oxygen makes up 21%
   C. Also about 10 other gases

II. Water
   A. Most water in air is in gas form (called water vapor)
   B. Amount of water in air is called humidity level
      1. 80%
         a. high level: lots of water in air
         b. probably feel uncomfortable
      2. 50%
         a. less water in air
         b. most people feel comfortable
      3. 10%
         a. deserts + other arid places
         b. not much water in air
      4. Percentage humidity shows how much of total possible amount of water is in air
   C. Sources of water
      1. most obvious = precipitation
      2. ocean + rivers
      3. trees + plants
      4. ground

LECTURE, PART TWO: Particulate Matter

GUESSING VOCABULARY FROM CONTEXT

Answers to step 2 (Student's Book page 88)

1 e, **2** d, **3** f, **4** a, **5** c, **6** b

Sample answers to step 2 (Student's Book page 89)

Types of particulate matter			
Natural		**Man-made**	
Source	**Particles**	**Action**	**Result**
volcano	smoke, ash	burning wood, bushes, or trees	more particulate matter added to air
forest fire	smoke, soot		
ocean waves	salt, sand	removing trees and water	easier for dust, dirt to be carried away and into air
flowers, trees, plants	pollen, natural matter		
carried by wind	dirt, dust	burning coal or other fossil fuels	more particulate matter added to air
(naturally occurring)	viruses, mold, bacteria		

AFTER THE LECTURE

APPLYING WHAT YOU HAVE LEARNED (Student's Book page 89)

Students' answers will vary.

Chapter 5 Lecture Quiz

See the Lecture Quiz section at the back of this Teacher's Manual for a photocopiable quiz on the lecture for Chapter 5. Quiz answers can be found on page 113.

Chapter 6

Weather and Climate

1 GETTING STARTED (Student's Book pages 90–92)

READING AND THINKING ABOUT THE TOPIC

Answers to step 2 (Student's Book page 91)

1 Weather is the state of the atmosphere at a certain time and place. Climate is the average weather over a period of time. The troposphere is the layer of the atmosphere closest to Earth's surface; most of Earth's weather is formed here.

2 This statement refers to climate. It means that the area where you live is dry most of the time, even if it rains occasionally.

3 Dry, tropical, mild, variable, polar

UNDERSTANDING SCIENTIFIC SYMBOLS

Answers to step 2 (Student's Book page 91)

1 rain showers
2 heavy snow
3 fog and drizzling rain
4 thunderstorm with hail

LISTENING FOR SPECIFIC INFORMATION

Answers to step 2 (Student's Book page 92)

1 The sky is clear and there are no clouds. Temperatures are warm.

2 The sky is dark and cloudy. The wind is strong. In about one hour, a thunderstorm will start.

3 The temperature is getting colder. The rain has changed to snow.

4 The heavy showers have ended, but there is still a lot of drizzle and fog.

Answers to step 3 (Student's Book page 92)

1 ○   2 ☿ (☊)   3 ✳   4 ♩

---

2 **AMERICAN VOICES: Sara, Dorothy, Yukiya, and Evylynn**
(Student's Book pages 93–97)

BEFORE THE INTERVIEWS

PERSONALIZING THE TOPIC (Student's Book page 93)
Answers to steps 2 and 3 will vary.

INTERVIEW WITH SARA: Meteorology

⌒ LISTENING FOR SPECIFIC INFORMATION

Answers to step 2 (Student's Book page 94)
Name: Sara
Country of origin: <u>Portugal</u>
Education: <u>graduate student, getting a Ph.D.</u>
She defines meteorology as a way of <u>describing</u> and trying to <u>understand</u> what happens in the <u>atmosphere</u>.
She decided to study meteorology because:
1 <u>Her father told her science was a good field</u>
2 <u>She has always been fascinated with the sky</u>

Answers to step 3 (Student's Book page 94)
The Earth is like <u>a big aquarium</u>.
Humans are like <u>fish</u>.
Our atmosphere is like <u>water</u>.

INTERVIEW WITH DOROTHY, YUKIYA, AND EVYLYNN: Severe weather

⌒ PREDICTING THE CONTENT

Answers to step 2 (Student's Book page 95)
Dorothy was in a <u>blizzard</u>.
Yukiya got caught in a <u>flood</u>.
Evylynn experienced a <u>hurricane</u>.

Answers to step 4 (Student's Book page 96)
1 E, **2** D, **3** E, **4** E, **5** Y, **6** D, **7** Y

🎧 LISTENING FOR OPINIONS

Answers (Student's Book page 96)

Do you think that global warming is affecting the weather on Earth?		Reasons for opinion
Sara	YES / NO / (DON'T KNOW)	Some changes may be caused by humans, but others may be natural. With science, until you have a definite answer, you don't know for sure.
Dorothy	(YES)/ NO / DON'T KNOW	Weather patterns have changed. For example, winters are much warmer than they used to be.
Yukiya	(YES)/ NO / DON'T KNOW	Ice and glaciers are melting in Antarctica. This is causing the ocean level to rise, which causes more hurricanes.
Evylynn	(YES)/ NO / DON'T KNOW	Global warming causes worse weather and more dangerous storms. Humans are changing Earth, and these changes affect the weather.

AFTER THE INTERVIEWS

UNDERSTANDING HUMOR ABOUT THE TOPIC (Student's Book page 97)

Students' answers will vary.

3 IN YOUR OWN VOICE (Student's Book page 98)

CONDUCTING A SURVEY

Survey results will vary.

4 ACADEMIC LISTENING AND NOTE TAKING: Global Warming

(Student's Book pages 99–104)

BEFORE THE LECTURE

BUILDING BACKGROUND KNOWLEDGE

Answers to step 2 (Student's Book page 99)

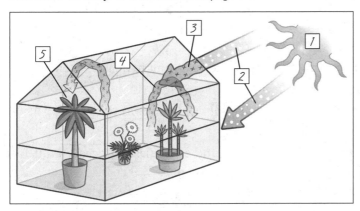

🎧 NOTE TAKING: LISTENING FOR NUMERICAL INFORMATION

Answers to step 2 (Student's Book page 100)

1 4.6 billion years
2 45%
3 1°C

4 100 years
5 90%

LECTURE, PART ONE: *The Greenhouse Effect*

GUESSING VOCABULARY FROM CONTEXT

Answers to step 2 (Student's Book page 101)
1 d, **2** b, **3** c, **4** a, **5** e

🎧 NOTE TAKING: COPYING A LECTURER'S ILLUSTRATIONS

Sample answers to step 2 (Student's Book page 101)

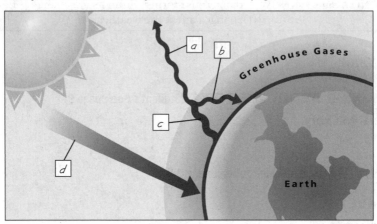

LECTURE, PART TWO: *Effects of Global Warming*

GUESSING VOCABULARY FROM CONTEXT

Answers to step 2 (Student's Book page 102)
1 f, **2** a, **3** d, **4** h, **5** b, **6** g, **7** e, **8** c

🎧 NOTE TAKING: LISTENING FOR CAUSE AND EFFECT

Sample answers to steps 1 and 2 (Student's Book page 103)

1 "Some of this rise is due to the heating of the ocean surface. As the oceans warm, they expand and sea level goes up."

    oceans warm → oceans exp → sea lev ↑

2 "The melt water is entering the ocean and resulting in a rise in sea level."

    melt H_2O enters ocean → sea lev ↑

3 "A second consequence of global warming is changes in the weather itself."

    glob warmg → chgs in wea

4 "Hurricanes develop over warm oceans, and so the rise in ocean temperatures may cause more and perhaps stronger hurricanes."

    ↑ ocean temps → more & strgr hurrics

THINKING CRITICALLY ABOUT THE TOPIC (Student's Book page 104)

Students' answers to step 2 will vary.

Chapter 6 Lecture Quiz

See the Lecture Quiz section at the back of this Teacher's Manual for a photocopiable quiz on the lecture for Chapter 6. Quiz answers can be found on page 114.

Additional Ideas for Unit 3

Key topics in this unit include the composition of the atmosphere, aspects of air quality (including humidity, aridity, particulate matter, and pollution), weather and climate, and global warming.

1 Watch a movie in class about severe weather, for example: *Twister* or *The Perfect Storm*. Alternatively, watch a movie about the effects of global warming, either from a fictional (*The Day After Tomorrow*) or non-fictional (*An Inconvenient Truth*) perspective. Have students discuss how the movies relate to the information they learned in the unit.

2 For listening practice, show authentic TV or online weather reports in class. Have students discuss the information they hear. As a follow-up, assign different students each week to give a brief weather report at the beginning of the class period.

3 Have groups of students research the history of weather patterns in a particular country or area. Students should note any changes in weather or climate over time and speculate on possible causes.

4 Have students research and report on a famous contemporary or past weather event, such as Hurricane Andrew, Hurricane Katrina, Hurricane Ike, the Dust Bowl period, or the 1900 hurricane in Galveston, Texas.

5 Have students work in groups and prepare a role play in which they imagine how they would react in a severe weather event, such as a hurricane or flood. Students can take various roles: people escaping from the event, first responders, newscasters covering the event, and so on.

6 Explore online resources related to the unit. NASA has a climate time machine and other interactive features at http://www.nasa.gov/multimedia/mmgallery/index.html. The website of the National Oceanic and Atmospheric Administration (NOAA) at http://www.noaa.gov/wx.html has an online weather tracker, national weather warnings and forecasts, live satellite images of weather patterns, and other educational features.

7 Explore the presence of weather in language by introducing expressions that include weather or atmosphere-related terms (for example: "I'm feeling under the weather"; "He has his head in the clouds"; "Every cloud has a silver lining"; or "There's a cloud on the horizon"). Alternatively, bring in or have students bring in songs in English about the weather, for example: *November Rain*, *Don't Let the Sun Go Down on Me*, *Soak up the Sun*, or *Through the Rain*). Listen to the song, study the lyrics, and discuss why the songwriter chose the words.

Life on Earth

Unit title page (Student's Book page 105)

Read the unit title and look at the opening photo collage. Ask students to identify all of the living things in the photos and share anything they know about the different organisms, such as their habitats or unique characteristics. Have students categorize the organisms into plants and animals, and then think of additional examples in both categories. Finally, have students brainstorm ways that plants and animals are similar, and ways that they are different. List the students' ideas on the board.

Read the unit opener and point out the key word *biosphere* and its definition. Chapter 7 is about plants and animals and the life processes that they share. Have students predict the life processes – the seven actions that all living things do. Chapters 8 and 9 focus exclusively on humans. Make sure that students know the meaning of the terms *nutrition*, *body system*, and *DNA*. Ask them to express their ideas about how exercise, nutrition, and DNA contribute to good health and longevity.

Chapter 7

Plants and Animals

1 **GETTING STARTED** (Student's Book pages 106–108)

READING AND THINKING ABOUT THE TOPIC

Answers to step 2 (Student's Book page 107)

1 Scientists have identified more than 1.5 million more animal species than plant species on Earth.

2 Plants and animals move, grow, use food and water to make energy, react to their environments, reproduce, and are interconnected with each other.

LISTENING FOR SPECIFIC INFORMATION

Answers to step 1 (Student's Book page 107)

1 blue whale	**2** Venus flytrap	**3** platypus
4 Giant Sequoia tree	**5** Goliath beetle	**6** bamboo

Answers to steps 3 and 4 (Student's Book page 108)

Organism	Habitat (where it lives)	Interesting facts
1 Giant Sequoia tree	California, U.S.	• largest species of tree on Earth • can be more than 100 m tall, 17 m wide
2 Blue whale	deep oceans	• largest animal in world (maybe in history of Earth) • can grow up to 33 m long, 150 tons • heart = size of small car
3 Bamboo	many diff climates, incl cold mtns & hot tropical jungles	• not tree but grass • fastest growing plant on Earth • can grow 4 cm in 1 hr

4 Platypus	Australia	• unusual looking – like duck w/ wide, flat tail • lives on land but good swimmer • lays eggs instead of giving birth to babies
5 Venus flytrap	Natural habit = southern U.S., but now all over world	• carnivorous (eats meat) • leaves snap shut when insect touches them – digests insect • popular houseplant
6 Goliath beetle	beetles live everywhere on Earth, except ocean and polar regions	• 95% of animal species = insects • 50% of insects = beetles (so far, 350,000 species) • Goliath largest & heaviest insect

2 AMERICAN VOICES: Frank, Vickie, and Reggie
(Student's Book pages 109–113)

BEFORE THE INTERVIEWS

PERSONALIZING THE TOPIC (Student's Book page 109)
Students' answers will vary.

BUILDING BACKGROUND KNOWLEDGE

Answers to step 2 (Student's Book page 109)
a Bee eats the nectar of a flower; spreads pollen so flower can reproduce.
b Clownfish hides in anemone and is protected from predators; anemone eats fish that clownfish attracts.
c Plover cleans food from crocodile's teeth; plover eats food in teeth.
d Ostrich has excellent eyesight, but poor sense of smell and hearing; zebra has excellent sense of smell and hearing, but poor eyesight. They travel together and warn each other of danger.

INTERVIEW WITH FRANK AND VICKIE: A green thumb
LISTENING FOR SPECIFIC INFORMATION

Answers to step 2 (Student's Book page 111)

	Frank	**Vickie**
How he or she became interested in gardening	In the 1930s and 1940s, everybody had <u>gardens</u>.	In the 1970s, everyone was trying to <u>grow their own food</u>. She was good at it and enjoyed it.
Favorite kind of plant to grow now	He likes to grow <u>native</u> plants.	She likes to grow <u>perennials</u>, which are plants that come back year after year.
What he or she likes about plants and gardening	He likes the challenge of finding and <u>collecting</u> the plants. He likes <u>sharing</u> plants with other people most of all.	It helps her to forget <u>day-to-day</u> <u>troubles</u>. It also makes her feel <u>connected</u> to the Earth.

INTERVIEW WITH REGGIE: *The Galapagos Islands*

🎧 LISTENING FOR EXAMPLES

Answers to steps 1 and 2 (Student's Book page 112)

1 You don't have to go far before you see wildlife. (For example) / For instance,) d

2 I got to see a lot of animals. Many different kinds of birds, (such as / like) a

3 There's been a lot of environmental damage already, so the idea that it's an untouched environment is wrong. (Let me give you an example:) / For example,) b

4 Any ecosystem is so tightly bound together that even one small thing can change the balance and destroy the system. (For example, / For instance,) c

AFTER THE INTERVIEWS

EXAMINING GRAPHIC MATERIAL

Answers to step 2 (Student's Book page 113)

1 Plants had the most threatened species in 2007. Amphibians had the highest percentage of threatened species in 2007.

2 Plants had the greatest increase of threatened species in 2007 (2,836 more threatened species since 2000). Some reasons for this change are: loss of habitat, changes to the water supply, climate change, invasive species that serve as competitors or predators, and human disturbance. Mammals are the only group that has fewer threatened species in 2007 than in 2000. This may be due to increased conservation efforts.

3 Answers will vary.

4 Answers will vary.

THINKING CRITICALLY ABOUT THE TOPIC (Student's Book page 113)

Students' answers will vary.

3 IN YOUR OWN VOICE (Student's Book pages 114–115)

CONDUCTING AN INTERVIEW

Students' questions, interview results, and reports will vary.

4 ACADEMIC LISTENING AND NOTE TAKING: What Is a Living Thing? (Student's Book pages 116–121)

BEFORE THE LECTURE

PREVIEWING THE TOPIC

Answers to step 3 (Student's Book page 116)

excretion: removal of waste materials from a living organism (separating waste materials from the body)

growth: increase in size

movement: change from one place or position to another

nutrition: the process of getting food

reproduction: the process of making more of the same organism

respiration: the process of changing food into energy by using oxygen (animals get the oxygen they need by breathing)

sensitivity: feeling and reacting to the environment

🎧 NOTE TAKING: LISTENING FOR EXPRESSIONS OF CONTRAST

Answers to steps 1 and 3 (Student's Book page 117)

1 Plants, for example, grow taller and wider throughout their lives. Animals start growing as soon as they are born, but unlike plants, usu stop growing when adults.

2 I'm sure you can think of many examples of different kinds of animal movement . . . . Plants move, too, but not in same way as animals.

3 Animals take in information about their environment by using their senses . . . . Although plants do not have as many senses as animals, they do react to H_2O, light.

4 Plants have a very special way of getting food – they make it themselves . . . . Animals, on the other hand, can't make own food.

5 Respiration is a way of changing food into energy by using oxygen. Animals take in oxygen by breathing in air, whereas plants have tiny holes in leaves.

6 During reproduction, plants and animals make more of their own kind. Animals have babies or lay eggs. In contrast, most plants make seeds.

LECTURE, PART ONE: Growth, Movement, and Sensitivity

GUESSING VOCABULARY FROM CONTEXT

Answers to step 2 (Student's Book page 118)

1 c, 2 a, 3 f, 4 e, 5 d, 6 b

🎧 NOTE TAKING: CHECKING YOUR NOTES

Sample answers to step 2 (Student's Book page 119)

Life process	Plants	Animals
Growth (size ↑)	grow taller & wider t/out life	start at birth – stop growing ~~when they die~~ when adults
Movement	– move roots ↓ into E., stems + lvs ↑ to sky – flwrs open + close – ~~faster~~ than anim mvmt slower	ex walk, run, fly, swim, crawl
	both P&A move to get food, place to live, esc from danger	
Sensitivity (sensitive to envir)	– ~~more~~ senses than anim fewer – react to stimuli, ex H_2O, light – sunflwr fall ~~moon~~ sun – V. flytrap – reacts when touched	– senses: see, hear, smell, taste, ~~talk~~ feel – use to get info + react to envir

LECTURE, PART TWO: Nutrition, Respiration, Excretion, and Reproduction

GUESSING VOCABULARY FROM CONTEXT

Answers to step 2 (Student's Book page 120)
1 b, **2** c, **3** a, **4** d

🎧 NOTE TAKING: ORGANIZING YOUR NOTES IN A CHART

Sample answers to step 2 (Student's Book page 120)

Life process	Plants	Animals
Nutrition (getting food)	– make own food – photosynthesis C_O2 + H_2O + sunlight = food	– cannot make own food – ∴ eat plants, other anim
Respiration (food → energy using O_2)	– get O_2 thru holes in lvs	– get O_2 by breathing
Excretion (remove waste)	– thru holes in lvs – roots – move waste to leaf → falls off	– breath, sweat, urine, feces
Reproduction (make more of own kind, nec to cont species)	– seeds	– babies – eggs

AFTER THE LECTURE

APPLYING WHAT YOU HAVE LEARNED

Answers to step 1 (Student's Book page 121)
Sunflower: All processes checked. Yes, it is living.

Fire: Answers may vary. Students will probably check movement and growth, and may also check sensitivity (a fire reacts to stimuli, such as wind); nutrition (it could be argued that fire "eats" wood or another energy source, although these nutrients are not ingested because fire has no cell structure); respiration (fire uses oxygen to convert its "food" into light and heat energy); and excretion (smoke, ash). However, fire cannot reproduce because it has no DNA or other genetic material to pass on. No, fire is not living.

Answers to step 3 (Student's Book page 121)
1 reproduction
2 growth, movement
3 sensitivity, movement, nutrition
4 respiration, excretion
5 sensitivity, nutrition

Chapter 7 Lecture Quiz

See the Lecture Quiz section at the back of this Teacher's Manual for a photocopiable quiz on the lecture for Chapter 7. Quiz answers can be found on page 114.

Chapter 8

The Human Body

1 GETTING STARTED (Student's Book pages 122–124)

READING AND THINKING ABOUT THE TOPIC

Answers to step 2 (Student's Book page 123)

1 Movement, growth, and reproduction are three life processes that are mentioned in the passage.

2 The picture on the left shows the skeletal system. Its role is to provide structure to the body. The picture on the right shows the muscular system. Its role is to enable and control movement of the body.

🎧 LISTENING TO DIRECTIONS

Answers to step 1 (Student's Book pages 123–124)

Task 1　b　　　　　　　　　　Task 3　Answers will vary.
Task 2　Answers will vary.　　Task 4　Answers will vary.

Answers to step 3 (Student's Book page 124)

　3　 Task 1　　　1　 Task 3
　4　 Task 2　　　2　 Task 4

2 AMERICAN VOICES: Becca and Louise (Student's Book pages 125–130)

BEFORE THE INTERVIEWS

PERSONALIZING THE TOPIC (Student's Book page 125)

Answers to steps 1 and 2 will vary.

BUILDING BACKGROUND KNOWLEDGE

Answers to step 2 (Student's Book page 126)
swimming <u>AE</u>
weight training <u>AN</u>
bicycling <u>AE</u>
yoga <u>AN</u>
push-ups <u>AN</u>
jogging <u>AE</u>

Answers to step 3 will vary.

INTERVIEW WITH BECCA: Experiences of a track athlete

🎧 LISTENING FOR MAIN IDEAS

Answers to step 2 (Student's Book page 127)
1, 2, 4, 5, 7

Answers to step 3 (Student's Book page 127)
<u>5</u> brings in more oxygen for the muscles
<u>3</u> helps the body remember the best positions for running
<u>7</u> makes bones stronger
<u>4</u> builds anaerobic power
<u>1</u> builds up the lungs and strengthens the heart
<u>4, 1</u> builds muscle strength
<u>1, 3, 4</u> makes the cardiovascular system work more efficiently

INTERVIEW WITH LOUISE: Eat to live; don't live to eat

🎧 LISTENING FOR SPECIFIC INFORMATION

Answers to step 2 (Student's Book page 128)
Fiber <u>c</u>   Protein <u>f</u>   Carbohydrates <u>b</u>
Fat <u>d</u>   Calcium <u>e</u>   Vitamin D <u>a</u>

AFTER THE INTERVIEWS

CONDUCTING A SURVEY (Student's Book page 129)

Answers will vary.

CONSIDERING RELATED INFORMATION

Answers to step 1 (Student's Book page 130)
1 Grains, vegetables, and milk and dairy products. Students' answers may include: grains provide the body with carbohydrates, the main source of energy for the body; vegetables are rich in nutrients and low in fat and calories; milk and dairy products are sources of calcium, vitamin D, and protein.

2 Oils. Food in this group are good for the body if consumed in small quantities, but can cause health problems (for example, weight gain, high cholesterol, cardiovascular disease, diabetes) if consumed in excess.

3 The person climbing stairs represents physical activity. Along with good nutrition, regular exercise is necessary to keep the body healthy. Another possible interpretation is that people can improve their physical health step by step by making small changes in their diet and lifestyle.

4 Answers will vary.

Answers to step 2 will vary.

3 IN YOUR OWN VOICE (Student's Book page 131)

SHARING YOUR OPINION

Students' answers will vary.

4 ACADEMIC LISTENING AND NOTE TAKING: Three Systems of the Human Body (Student's Book pages 132–138)

BEFORE THE LECTURE

BUILDING BACKGROUND KNOWLEDGE AND VOCABULARY

Answers to step 1 (Student's Book page 132)

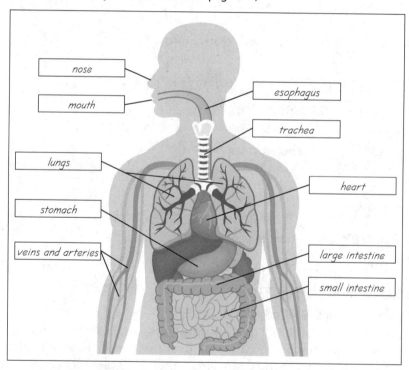

nose

mouth

esophagus

trachea

lungs

heart

stomach

veins and arteries

large intestine

small intestine

Answers to step 2 (Student's Book page 133)

1 The arteries carry blood from the heart to the body.
The esophagus connects the mouth and stomach. Food travels down the esophagus to the stomach during digestion.

The heart is the source of power for the cardiovascular system. It pumps blood through the entire body.

The large intestine absorbs water from food during digestion. The water goes into the body, and the remaining waste in the intestine is removed from the body by excretion.

The lungs are where oxygen from inhaled air passes into the body, and carbon dioxide (waste produced during cell activity) passes from the body into the lungs, to be exhaled in our breath.

The mouth takes in air during the process of respiration and helps break down food during the process of digestion.

The nose brings air into the body during respiration; it is also the primary organ for the sense of smell.

The small intestine absorbs nutrients from digested food and passes them into the blood.

The stomach is where food is broken down so that the body can absorb water and nutrients from the food.

The trachea connects the mouth and nose to the lungs and serves as a passage for inhaled and exhaled air.

The veins carry blood from the body back to the heart.

2 The nose, trachea, lungs, and mouth are part of the respiratory system. The large intestine, esophagus, mouth, small intestine, and stomach are part of the digestive system. The arteries, veins, and heart are part of the cardiovascular system.

🎧 NOTE TAKING: LISTENING FOR EXPRESSIONS OF TIME ORDER

Answers to step 2 (Student's Book page 133)

1 This phase can last for several hours, and <u>when</u> it's over, the food has become a thick soup.

2 From the stomach, the food <u>then</u> moves into the small intestine, where something very important happens.

3 <u>Finally</u>, the remaining dry waste, or feces, moves out of the large intestine and out of the body.

4 When we breathe, air enters our body through our mouth and nose. <u>Next</u>, it travels through an airway called the trachea into the lungs.

5 <u>After</u> entering our blood, oxygen is transported to every part of the body, where our cells use it to carry out life functions.

6 <u>Finally</u>, the oxygenated blood returns to the heart, ready to begin the cycle again.

LECTURE, PART ONE: The Digestive System

GUESSING VOCABULARY FROM CONTEXT

Answers to step 2 (Student's Book page 134)

1 g, 2 a, 3 e, 4 c, 5 f, 6 d, 7 b

Sample answers to step 2 (Student's Book page 135)

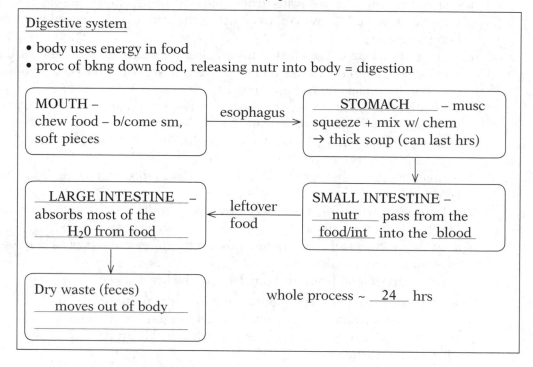

Digestive system

- body uses energy in food
- proc of bkng down food, releasing nutr into body = digestion

MOUTH –
chew food – b/come sm,
soft pieces

→ esophagus →

STOMACH – musc
squeeze + mix w/ chem
→ thick soup (can last hrs)

LARGE INTESTINE –
absorbs most of the
H$_2$0 from food

← leftover food ←

SMALL INTESTINE –
nutr pass from the
food/int into the blood

Dry waste (feces)
moves out of body

whole process ~ 24 hrs

LECTURE, PART TWO: The Respiratory and Cardiovascular Systems

GUESSING VOCABULARY FROM CONTEXT

Answers to step 2 (Student's Book page 136)
1 e, 2 h, 3 b, 4 g, 5 f, 6 i, 7 a, 8 c, 9 d

⌒ **NOTE TAKING: TAKING NOTES IN A FLOW CHART**

Answers to step 1 will vary. (Student's Book page 137)

Sample answers to step 3 (Student's Book page 137)

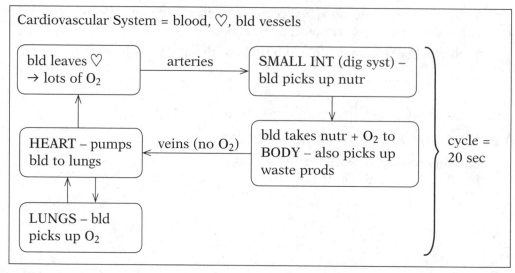

Cardiovascular System = blood, ♡, bld vessels

bld leaves ♡
→ lots of O$_2$

→ arteries →

SMALL INT (dig syst) –
bld picks up nutr

HEART – pumps
bld to lungs

← veins (no O$_2$) ←

bld takes nutr + O$_2$ to
BODY – also picks up
waste prods

LUNGS – bld
picks up O$_2$

cycle =
20 sec

USING YOUR NOTES TO LABEL AN ILLUSTRATION (Student's Book page 138)

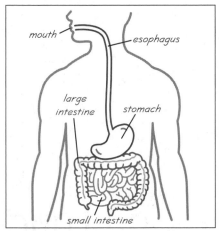

The Digestive System

Arrows should show food coming in the mouth, going down the esophagus and into the stomach. From the stomach, food goes into the small intestine, then the large intestine, and then it is eliminated from the body.

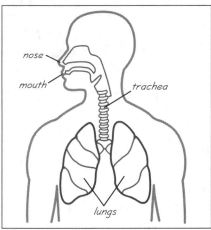

The Respiratory System

Arrows should show that air enters the body through the nose and mouth. It travels through the trachea into the lungs. Inside the lungs, oxygen in the air passes into the blood and travels to all parts of the body; carbon dioxide from the blood passes back into the lungs and then travels into the trachea to be exhaled through the nose and mouth.

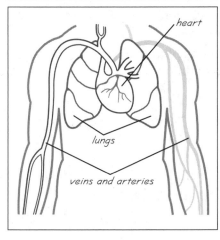

The Cardiovascular System

Arrows should show that blood travels from the heart to the arteries, which carry the blood all over the body. When the oxygen in the blood has been used up, the veins carry it back to the heart. It is immediately pumped into the lungs to get fresh oxygen from the respiratory system. The oxygenated blood returns to the heart to begin the cycle again.

Chapter 8 Lecture Quiz

See the Lecture Quiz section at the back of this Teacher's Manual for a photocopiable quiz on the lecture for Chapter 8. Quiz answers can be found on page 114.

Chapter 9

Living Longer, Living Better?

1 **GETTING STARTED** (Student's Book pages 139–141)

READING AND THINKING ABOUT THE TOPIC

Answers to step 2 (Student's Book page 140)

1 Life expectancy is the number of years a person is expected to live, whereas life span is the longest number of years any person has ever lived.

2 According to the passage, the average world life expectancy was 30 years in 1900, and then increased by three years every ten years. Therefore, in 1950, the average world life expectancy was about 45 years.

3 Genetic research may enable scientists to understand and prevent common diseases like cancer and heart disease. In addition, it may help scientists slow the aging process.

🎧 RECORDING AND CALCULATING NUMBERS (Student's Book page 141)

Students' answers will vary.

2 AMERICAN VOICES: Anna, Jericho, and Eleanor
(Student's Book pages 142–146)

BEFORE THE INTERVIEWS

SHARING YOUR OPINION (Student's Book page 142)

Students' answers will vary.

INTERVIEW WITH ANNA: The disadvantages of aging

🎧 LISTENING FOR DETAILS

Answers to step 1 (Student's Book page 143)

Factors that increase longevity: medical advances, education, better preparation for old age, better nutrition

Disadvantages of getting older: can't see well, loss of independence, can't walk well, bigger risk of disease

Answers to step 2 (Student's Book page 143)

1 Yes, she's sure they will figure it out.

2 Maybe. If a person is healthy, then extending the life span is a good idea. But if a person is not healthy, then extending the life span is not a benefit.

3 Maybe. Only if she is in good health and the years between 90–100 are quality years.

INTERVIEW WITH JERICHO: Extending the human life span

🎧 LISTENING FOR SPECIFIC INFORMATION

Answers to step 2 (Student's Book page 145)

1 a, **2** c, **3** b, **4** a

INTERVIEW WITH ELEANOR: Looking forward to the future

🎧 LISTENING FOR SPECIFIC INFORMATION

Answers to step 2 (Student's Book page 146)

Eleanor is 81 years old. She stays active. For example, she is a member of several organizations, clubs. She likes to talk with other people. Sometimes she takes a class at the university. She loves to read. Most of all, she likes to spend time with her family.

During Eleanor's lifetime, the world population has gone from 2 billion to 6 billion. She thinks overpopulation is the number one problem facing the world. There isn't enough food and housing for all the people in the world.

Eleanor hopes the future will be a better place. She got her positive attitude from her father, who was always trying to help the young people of the world. Eleanor would love to be here 100 years from now to see what the world is like.

AFTER THE INTERVIEWS

EXAMINING GRAPHIC MATERIAL

Answers (Student's Book page 146)

1 Life expectancy is highest in North America and lowest in sub-Saharan Africa.

2 The greatest change has been in Asia, where average life expectancy has increased by 26 years since 1950.

3 Sub-Saharan Africa is the only region where life expectancy is moving downward. Students' ideas about why this is so may vary. The number one cause is the HIV/AIDS epidemic, but additional factors include other diseases, lack of public access to health care, poor sanitation, and poor nutrition – common problems that affect poorer nations.

4 Answers will vary.

3 IN YOUR OWN VOICE (Student's Book page 147)

THINKING CRITICALLY ABOUT THE TOPIC

Answers to step 1 (Student's Book page 147)

Extending the human life span	
For	Against
• You can see your children and grandchildren grow up. • You can see society change. • There are many exciting and interesting things coming up in the future.	• If the process is expensive, only rich people will be able to extend their lives. • It's not a benefit if the person is not in good health. • It just delays the inevitable.

Answers to steps 2 and 3 will vary.

4 ACADEMIC LISTENING AND NOTE TAKING: DNA and the Human Life Span (Student's Book pages 148–155)

BEFORE THE LECTURE

PERSONALIZING THE TOPIC (Student's Book page 148)

Students' answers will vary.

BUILDING BACKGROUND KNOWLEDGE AND VOCABULARY

Answers to step 2 (Student's Book page 149)

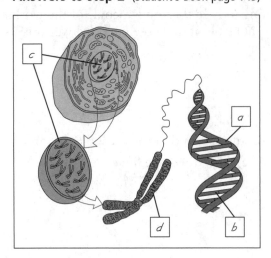

🎧 NOTE TAKING: LISTENING FOR SPECULATIVE LANGUAGE

Answers to step 2 (Student's Book page 150)

1 Of course, the environment that you grow up in and your lifestyle (apparently influence /(also influence)) things like your body shape and your personality . . .

2 Scientists also ((think that genes may)/ know that genes) also play a role in determining how long we can live.

3 In 2003, a group of international scientists called the Human Genome Organization (seems to have succeeded /(succeeded)) in analyzing human DNA for the first time.

4 For example, the scientists learned which specific genes carry diseases . . . . By studying the human genome more, they ((might)/ will) soon find ways to treat and even prevent these diseases.

5 But many researchers (know /(believe)) that gene therapy will soon become a common way of preventing and curing disease.

6 Studies of certain insects, worms, and mice have found genes that ((seem to allow)/ allow) these organisms to live longer.

LECTURE, PART ONE: What is DNA?

GUESSING VOCABULARY FROM CONTEXT

Answers to step 2 (Student's Book page 150)
1 e, **2** b, **3** d, **4** g, **5** c, **6** f, **7** a

🎧 NOTE TAKING: EVALUATING YOUR OWN NOTE TAKING (Student's Book page 151)

Students' answers will vary.

LECTURE, PART TWO: Can DNA Extend the Human Life Span?

GUESSING VOCABULARY FROM CONTEXT

Answers to step 2 (Student's Book page 152)
1 a, **2** e, **3** d, **4** f, **5** c, **6** b

🎧 NOTE TAKING: LISTENING FOR RHETORICAL QUESTIONS

Sample answers to step 2 (Student's Book page 153)

1 Genes carry information about what kinds of diseases a person is likely to get. They may also play a role in determining how long a person lives. By studying genes and DNA, scientists can learn more about how to expand the human life span.

2 When scientists find a gene in a person that increases his or her chances of getting a particular disease, they can replace that gene with a new gene that does not carry the disease. This reduces the person's likelihood of getting sick.

3 There probably is, based on research that shows that longevity is to some degree inherited.

CONSIDERING RELATED INFORMATION

Answers to step 5 (Student's Book page 154)

Dominant traits: free earlobes, dimples, can roll tongue, widow's peak

Recessive traits: attached earlobes, no dimples, cannot roll tongue, straight hairline

UNDERSTANDING HUMOR ABOUT THE TOPIC

Answers to step 2 (Student's Book page 155)

1 A money tree
2 Genetic engineering is seen as a good thing.
3 Students' answers will vary.
4 Students' answers will vary.

Chapter 9 Lecture Quiz

See the Lecture Quiz section at the back of this Teacher's Manual for a photocopiable quiz on the lecture for Chapter 9. Quiz answers can be found on page 114.

Additional Ideas for Unit 4

This unit looks at the definition of a living thing, and surveys life on Earth with a particular focus on plants, animals, and humans. Other key topics include the systems of the human body and keeping healthy through nutrition and exercise. The unit also considers human aging and the role that DNA may play in extending the human life span.

1 Some movies that relate to the themes in this unit are: *WALL-E*, an animated film about a future Earth, which has become so polluted by human activity that it can no longer support any living things; *AI*, a science fiction movie whose main character is a human-like boy who wants to become a real human; *Tuck Everlasting*, in which a 15-year-old girl is given the option of drinking from a fountain that will allow her to live forever.

2 Invite a guest speaker to your class to talk about a topic related to the unit. Possible speakers could include a botanist, a zoologist, a veterinarian, a medical doctor or other healthcare professional, an athlete, nutritionist, or dietician.

3 Explain to students that food chains and food webs show the relationship among living things in a particular ecosystem, and how energy is passed from one living thing to another. Give an example of one food chain or web and have students think of other examples. Then discuss how the organisms in the ecosystem depend on each other, and what would happen if any one of the organisms were eliminated from the web.

4 Have students grow their own plant at school or at home. Students should observe and note changes in the plant on a daily basis, and describe how the plant reacts to stimuli such as water and light.

5 Assign each student or groups of students a common but little understood bodily function, such as yawning, sneezing, coughing, stomach growling, burping, or hiccuping. Students should do research and find out what causes these involuntary actions, and what is happening in the human body when they take place. As a class, discuss how these functions relate to the human systems discussed in the unit.

6 Ask students to bring in labels from foods they have eaten recently. In groups, have them analyze the information on the label. Some of the questions you may want them to answer include: Which food group does the item belong to? What nutrients does it have? What health benefits does it provide for the body?

7 Have students research the historical events that allowed the human life span to expand so dramatically in the nineteenth and twentieth centuries. They can investigate developments in sanitation, nutrition, food processing, and transportation, as well as the introduction of antibiotics and other medical advances. Have students create a timeline with the information they learn.

8 Ask students to interview active, healthy people they know who are in their 80s and 90s. Students should find out how these seniors stay healthy – whether it is due to lifestyle choices, genetic factors, or a combination of the two.

Listening Script

Listening Script

Narrator: *Academic Listening Encounters: The Natural World*
Listening, Note Taking, and Discussion
by Yoneko Kanaoka
Series editor: Bernard Seal
Published by Cambridge University Press
This audio program contains the listening material for the *Academic Listening Encounters: The Natural World* Student's Book.
This recording is copyright.

1

Narrator: CD 1
Chapter 1, The Physical Earth
Page 3
Listening to Directions, Step 2
When you hear the word *pause*, **stop the recording and follow the instructions.**

Man: Look at the diagram in your book. It shows some of the planets in our solar system. All of the planets in our solar system move around the Sun. Find the Sun in the diagram. Color the Sun yellow. Pause . . . . The two planets closest to the sun are Mercury and Venus. Because they are so close to the Sun, these planets are very hot. Earth is the third planet from the Sun. Find the place for Earth in your picture and draw a circle. Label the circle "Earth" – E-a-r-t-h. Earth is often called the "Blue Planet" because there is so much water on its surface. Color the Earth blue in your picture. Pause . . . . The next planet after Earth is Mars. Mars is smaller than Earth, so draw a small circle on your picture. Label the circle "Mars" – M-a-r-s. Mars is sometimes called the "Red Planet" because its surface is covered with rocks and soil that are reddish-orange. Color Mars red in your picture. Pause . . . . The fifth planet from the sun is Jupiter. Jupiter is the largest planet in our solar system,

so draw a big circle for Jupiter. Label the circle "Jupiter" – J-u-p-i-t-e-r. Pause . . . . Jupiter, Saturn, Uranus, and Neptune are all gas planets. These planets are all very cold because they are far away from the Sun. All four of these planets have rings, or circular bands of matter that move around the planet. Saturn's rings are very broad and bright, so bright that they can be seen from Earth. In your picture, draw rings around the four gas planets. Draw thin rings around Jupiter, Uranus, and Neptune. Draw a thick ring around Saturn. Pause . . . .

Narrator: This concludes the task.

Narrator: Chapter 1, The Physical Earth
Page 6
Listening for Main Ideas in an Interview, Step 2

Interviewer: Brad, you're a geologist. Can you define "geology" for me?

Brad: Well, the simplest definition is the study of rocks. But it's more complicated than that. It's really the study of the composition and dynamics of the Earth, from its center to its surface. So geologists study what it's made of and how it moves.

Interviewer: How did you become interested in geology?

Brad: I guess there's something inside me that asks all these questions about the Earth. Like, the first time I saw the Rocky Mountains, these huge mountains, I had so many questions in my head: How could these mountains be here? What caused this? And when we had an earthquake in California I was curious: Why is the Earth shaking? When I was growing up, I was always interested in beaches: How do beaches get their shape, and why do they change? So, I've always been really interested in why things look the way they do and why things change on our planet.

Interviewer: It sounds like from a young age you had questions that led you to this area. I mean, it sounds like geology is a very good career for you.

Brad: Yes. I enjoy learning about it and I enjoy my work.

Interviewer: What are you working on right now?

Brad: Now, we go to beaches and take distance and height measurements of the shape of each beach, and we compare how the beach has changed from season to season and then from year to year.

Interviewer: And have you found that there is some change?

Brad: There's definitely change. There's change from winter to summer that has a big effect on the shape of the beaches. We see that every year. But what we're really looking for is a chronic erosion problem.

Interviewer: Does that mean there's too much erosion?

Brad: That's right. If the beaches don't come back year after year, they're eroding over time. That's the harder thing to measure.

Interviewer: Why should people care about geology?

Brad: First of all, it's just a lot of fun. You get to work outdoors. But second of all, it's important to our society. Humans have really taken over this planet and we're having a big effect on it, and it's important to understand what we're doing. So there are lots of reasons why people should be excited about geology.

Narrator: Now complete the steps in your book.

Narrator: Chapter 1, The Physical Earth
Page 8
Listening for Details, Step 2

Interviewer: Gaby, you've been to the Grand Canyon twice, right?

Gaby: Yes, I went hiking and camping there the first time, and the second time I got to ride in a helicopter and fly down into the canyon.

Interviewer: Would you say the Grand Canyon is one of the most famous natural landforms in the United States?

Gaby: Definitely!

Interviewer: What does it look like?

Gaby: Well, it's hard to describe because it's so big. When you stand there looking at it, it seems to go on forever. And there are all these cliffs that go down into the earth, and they're all different colors, like red and blue, purple and orange, yellow and brown. It almost looks like a painter came and just painted on a canvas.

Interviewer: I thought it wouldn't have much color, since it's formed out of rock.

Gaby: I thought so, too, but the cool thing is the colors of the stones are so different. And when the sun moves, it changes the colors of the canyon walls. So if you stand there for an hour, you can see the light changing on all the different rock formations. The same area looks totally different.

Interviewer: It sounds beautiful!

Gaby: It is. A lot of people say that when they see the Grand Canyon for the first time, it brings tears to their eyes, because it's so beautiful.

Interviewer: Did you have tears in your eyes?

Gaby: Well, I remember being like, this is one of the most beautiful things I've ever seen, and feeling very lucky to be experiencing it. And I remember thinking that it's something human beings could never create. I mean, it took millions of years!

Interviewer: How was it created?

Gaby: I think most of it was formed by water. The Colorado River goes through the floor of the Grand Canyon, and the water cut through the rock over millions of years. Basically, the canyon was eroded out of the earth by water.

Interviewer: So, Jane, tell me about a famous landform in Australia.

Jane: Right. Uluru is one of the most visited sites in my country. It's a massive, red sandstone rock in the center of Australia.

I've heard that its name means "island mountain." It's also called Ayers Rock.

Interviewer: So it was a mountain at one point?

Jane: Yeah. Well, millions of years ago layers of rock were lifted out of the earth. Then over time, the softer rocks eroded away and Uluru is what's left. It's made up of very, very hard minerals, mostly quartz and feldspar. We believe it's more than 300 million years old.

Interviewer: Incredible!

Jane: Australia is a unique place. We're the oldest continent. We're also the flattest, and the driest inhabited continent. We have a lot of unique and stunning natural landscapes.

Interviewer: What does Uluru look like?

Jane: It's beautiful! It's a large, red rock in the middle of a flat plain. From a distance it looks smooth, but up close, it looks like honeycomb. It's got holes, and it's quite rough. The surface is reddish-brown, but the color can change depending on the time of day. I've seen it look pink, purple, and sometimes gray. When the sun hits it, it looks like it's glowing.

Narrator: Now complete the steps in your book.

Narrator: Chapter 1, The Physical Earth Page 12
Listening for Main Ideas in a Lecture, Step 3

Narrator: Lecture topic.

Leslie Tamppari: Today, we'll be discussing the internal structure of Earth . . .

Narrator: First main idea.

Leslie Tamppari: But first, I want to give you some background information about our planet.

Narrator: Second main idea.

Leslie Tamppari: Now, I'd like to discuss each of the three main sections. First, the crust. The Earth's crust is what we see when we look at Earth's surface . . . . There are two kinds of crust, oceanic and continental.

Narrator: Third main idea.

Leslie Tamppari: Moving down from the crust, the next layer of the Earth is called the mantle.

Narrator: Fourth main idea.

Leslie Tamppari: Finally, continuing down toward the center of the planet, we come to the core. The Earth's core is a little thicker than the mantle and can be divided into two parts, an outer core and an inner core.

Narrator: Now complete the steps in your book.

Narrator: Chapter 1, The Physical Earth Page 14
Note Taking: Listening for Supporting Details, Step 3

Leslie Tamppari: When you think of the planet Earth, what do you think of? Probably the many natural features that you can see: mountains, forests, deserts, oceans, rivers and lakes, soil and rocks. But have you ever thought about what's *below* Earth's surface? What would we find if we cut the Earth in half and looked inside? Today, we'll be discussing the internal structure of Earth, and examining each of its three main sections: the crust, the mantle, and the core.

But first, I want to give you some background information about our planet. The Earth is about 4.6 billion years old. It's the third planet from the Sun, and the fifth largest in our solar system. If we draw a line directly through the center of the planet, the distance from the North Pole to the South Pole is almost 13,000 kilometers. It's the only planet in our solar system that has liquid water on its surface. In fact, 71 percent of the planet's surface is covered with water. Earth is also the densest planet in the solar system. Let's look at its internal structure more closely to find out what makes it so dense.

The Earth is made up of three main layers. The outer layer is called the crust. The next layer is called the mantle. The center of Earth is called the core. Scientists can guess what each layer is made of by studying seismic waves, or vibrations, that pass through the different layers. Seismic waves act differently as they pass through different kinds of materials, so these waves can tell scientists important information about the Earth's layers.

Narrator: Now complete the steps in your book.

Narrator: Chapter 1, The Physical Earth
Page 16
Note Taking: Listening for Supporting Details, Step 2

Leslie Tamppari: Now, I'd like to discuss each of the three main sections. First, the crust. The Earth's crust is what we see when we look at Earth's surface. If you imagine that Earth is a piece of fruit, the crust is like the skin of the fruit. Our planet's skin is made up of solid rock and is less dense than the mantle or the core. There are two kinds of crust, oceanic and continental. As I said before, you can only see about 30 percent of the Earth's crust. The rest is covered by oceans. The crust under water is called oceanic crust, and it's only about 6 to 11 kilometers thick.

The part of the crust that makes up Earth's land areas is called continental crust. It's thicker than oceanic crust, about 30 to 40 kilometers thick. The movement of Earth's crust causes earthquakes and the formation of natural land features, such as mountains and valleys.

Moving down from the crust, the next layer of the Earth is called the mantle. This layer is much thicker than the crust, and goes down to about 2,900 kilometers deep. It's also much denser than the crust, because most of the Earth's mass is located in the mantle. The upper part of the mantle is cool, solid rock, like the crust, but the further down you go, the more the temperature increases. And so the lower part of the mantle is hot and soft.

Finally, continuing down toward the center of the planet, we come to the core. The Earth's core is a little thicker than the mantle and can be divided into two parts, an outer core and an inner core. The outer core is extremely hot – so hot, in fact, that the rocks and minerals here melt and become liquid. Think about that! About 2,900 kilometers below us, there's a layer of liquid rock near the center of the Earth.

At the very center of the Earth there is a huge ball of very high pressure and high temperature material. This is called the inner core. Scientists believe the inner core is made of solid iron and nickel. These two metals together, plus the pressure of the rest of the Earth pushing down on it, create temperatures as high as 4,000 degrees Celsius. This heat moves outward from the core and heats the planet from the inside.

Narrator: Now complete the steps in your book.

2

Narrator: Chapter 2, The Dynamic Earth
Page 19
Listening for Numerical Information About Distances and Rates, Step 2

Man: The two large plates underneath the Atlantic Ocean are moving away from each other. Scientists have measured the rate of movement at 2 to 3 centimeters per year. In other words, the Atlantic Ocean is slowly growing bigger, by about 2.5 centimeters every year.

Woman: The Himalaya Mountains began to form when two continental plates pushed together 50 million years ago. As the two plates came together, the land was pushed up and formed mountains. Today, the plates are still moving toward each other, and the Himalayas are rising at a rate of about 5 millimeters per year.

Man: Sometimes two plates move past each other side by side. The San Andreas Fault in California is an example of this. The southern part of California is moving northwest, while the northern part of California is sliding southeast. The rate of movement is almost 5 centimeters per year. It probably won't happen, but in the future, San Francisco and Los Angeles could slide past each other.

Woman: The Hawaiian Islands are moving away from South America at a rate of about 7 centimeters per year. As they move northwest, they are getting closer and closer to Japan.

Narrator: Now complete the steps in your book.

**Narrator: Chapter 2, The Dynamic Earth
Page 22
Answering Multiple Choice Questions, Step 2**

Interviewer: Loren, you live on the Big Island of Hawaii, one of the most seismically active places on Earth.

Loren: I think the Big Island is *the* most seismically active. At least, we have the world's most active volcano. Kilauea has been erupting continuously since 1983.

Interviewer: What's it like living near an active volcano?

Loren: Exciting. I never get tired of watching it erupt. In the mid '80s, I was working at a school close to the volcano. I'll never forget standing on the second floor of the building and seeing a fountain of lava shoot 800 feet in the air.

Interviewer: You could see a fountain of lava from your school?

Loren: Yeah, 2,000-degree rock shooting straight up in the air. It was just spectacular. And the sound was so loud. Volcanoes make a really loud sound when they erupt – um, like a, like a jet taking off at the airport. It was awesome!

Interviewer: That does sound awesome.

Loren: And I felt lucky to see an active volcano. You know, not many people in the world have that opportunity.

Interviewer: And Kilauea is still erupting today?

Loren: Yeah, but a lot of the time, the lava flows underground. Sometimes you can see the bright orange lava flowing toward the ocean, and when the hot lava meets the ocean, it creates a big cloud of steam.

Interviewer: It's probably dangerous, but I would really like to see it.

Loren: Yeah, when there's an eruption, people do want to go and see it. But the volcanoes in Hawaii aren't the explosive type. People hurry to see active lava, from a distance, of course. It's beautiful.

Interviewer: I guess what they're seeing is the birth of land on Earth. That lava becomes the newest land on our planet.

Loren: Yeah, new land is always being formed. And scientists are watching Loihi now. It's a volcano in the ocean next to the Big Island. That hasn't yet come to the surface yet. Someday, it'll be the newest Hawaiian island.

Narrator: Now complete the steps in your book.

**Narrator: Chapter 2, The Dynamic Earth
Page 23
Drawing Inferences, Step 2**

Interviewer: Zack, you grew up in San Francisco, and Yoshiko, you grew up in Tokyo, and now you both live in San Francisco, right?

Zack and Yoshiko: Right.

Interviewer: So, you're both familiar with areas that have a lot of earthquakes. Could you tell me about your experiences with earthquakes?

Zack: Well, most earthquakes are very small, so typically you won't even know they've happened. Many earthquakes have happened when I was asleep and didn't even notice. And then there are small ones that happen very quickly and you think, "Oh, was that an earthquake?" That just feels like a little shaking.

Interviewer: Have you ever felt a really strong earthquake?

Zack: The biggest one I've felt, I was in a tall office building and it felt like the floor became liquid, you know, like there was a wave going through the room. And the corners of the office were going up and down like ocean waves.

Interviewer: Yoshiko, have you had similar experiences in Japan?

Yoshiko: Oh, yes. I don't remember every single earthquake I've had in Japan, but most of the ones I felt were when I was at home.

Interviewer: Oh, really?

Yoshiko: Yes, because if you're outside walking or driving, you're not going to notice an earthquake, unless it's a big one. But in my house, the furniture starts rattling. I hear the noise first; then I know an earthquake is starting.

Interviewer: Weren't you both afraid when these earthquakes happened?

Zack: Like I said, most of them are so small that it's no big deal. When you grow up in that kind of area, then it's just part of life. You get training in school, and hopefully you remember what to do if there's real danger.

Interviewer: What kind of training?

Zack: Well, in school, we had earthquake drills. Just like you have fire drills to prepare for a fire. Students get under their desks, and the teacher gets under the doorway.

Yoshiko: In Japan, when an earthquake starts, everybody starts opening doors so later we'll be able to go outside. And we know we should go under a desk or table, or in the bathroom. Also, we talk with our family and decide where we should go after an earthquake. Usually it's in the park or the school or some other open space.

Interviewer: So you make an emergency plan.

Zack: Right, because you need to be prepared for loss of electricity, loss of communication.

Interviewer: What are other things you do to prepare for an earthquake?

Yoshiko: We try to keep extra water at home.

Zack: Water is the number one thing. And then food is number two. Let's see, what else . . . a flashlight, extra batteries, a radio, extra blankets.

Interviewer: So, living in San Francisco, you're not afraid that "the big one" might be coming soon?

Zack: I think earthquakes are amazing – when you imagine how powerful that energy is, shaking a huge amount of space and land. But I love San Francisco, and it happens to have earthquakes, and so it's just part of life. Otherwise you couldn't live. I mean, you just have to live your life.

Narrator: Now complete the steps in your book.

Narrator: Chapter 2, The Dynamic Earth Page 24 Retelling What You Have Heard, Step 2

Interviewer: I know that there was a famous earthquake in Japan, the Kobe earthquake. Kei, were you living there in 1995, during the earthquake?

Kei: Yes, I was there. I'm from Nishinomiya, which is between Kobe and Osaka, so it's not really Kobe city but near Kobe.

Interviewer: Well, I know the Kobe earthquake struck Japan suddenly on January 17, 1995, and that it measured 7.2 on the Richter scale. It was a very powerful earthquake. What do you remember about that day?

Kei: When I think about the earthquake, I feel so sad, because I didn't lose any friends or family, but I had friends who lost their parents and their friends, so it's a very sad memory for me.

Interviewer: I understand.

Kei: It was five in the morning, and I was sleeping, and I felt this very strong shaking. In the beginning it was up and down, and then a couple of seconds later, it was side-to-side movement. It felt like such a long time! After that, our family gathered together in the living room. Everything had fallen, all the dishes, everything . . . and we could hear a woman screaming.

Interviewer: Someone was screaming?

Kei: Yes, our neighbor. She was stuck under a door.

Interviewer: Was she OK?

Kei: Yes, she was OK. Everyone in our neighborhood was OK. Our building didn't fall, but the stairs leading to our apartment fell down, so there were no more stairs. And the highway fell down, and many houses, too.

Interviewer: Everyone must have been panicking!

Kei: You know, not really. People were calm, and on that day, I didn't even feel scared. After the earthquake, though, life was difficult for a while.

Interviewer: What happened?

Kei: Well, the water didn't come on for two or three months . . . government trucks came every day to give out water. There were no trains, so I had to take my bike to pick up the water. We couldn't take a shower. For a long time, we didn't have gas or electricity, either. But I was lucky. I had a house and a family to take care of me. I was so grateful for that. Thousands of people lost their homes.

Interviewer: Are you afraid that something like the Kobe earthquake will happen again?

Kei: No. The memories are still very fresh, but I'm not afraid. I'm prepared, but I'm not afraid.

Narrator: Now complete the steps in your book.

Narrator: Chapter 2, The Dynamic Earth Page 29 Note Taking: Focusing on the Introduction, Step 1

Patricia Fryer: Today's lecture is going to be about volcanoes. I have loved volcanoes ever since I was a kid and I saw the active volcano Kilauea on the Big Island of Hawaii. I didn't know it then, but about 75 percent of all the rocks on the surface of the Earth are formed by volcanoes. Every day, there are about 20 volcanoes erupting on Earth. So, this is a really important topic when we talk about our natural world.

I'd like to start today's lecture by introducing the basic structure of a

volcano. Then I'll describe four basic types of volcanoes: shield volcanoes, composite volcanoes, cinder cone volcanoes, and supervolcanoes. For each basic type, I'll also give you an example. Finally, we'll discuss some of the signs scientists can look for before a volcanic eruption happens. So, let's get started.

Narrator: Now complete the steps in your book.

Narrator: Chapter 2, The Dynamic Earth Page 31 Note Taking: Using Telegraphic Language, Step 3

Patricia Fryer: Today's lecture is going to be about volcanoes. I have loved volcanoes ever since I was a kid and I saw the active volcano Kilauea on the Big Island of Hawaii. I didn't know it then, but about 75 percent of all the rocks on the surface of the Earth are formed by volcanoes. Every day, there are about 20 volcanoes erupting on Earth. So, this is a really important topic when we talk about our natural world.

I'd like to start today's lecture by introducing the basic structure of a volcano. Then I'll describe four basic types of volcanoes: shield volcanoes, composite volcanoes, cinder cone volcanoes, and supervolcanoes. For each basic type, I'll also give you an example. Finally, we'll discuss some of the signs scientists can look for before a volcanic eruption happens. So, let's get started.

First, the basic structure of a volcano. Well, volcanoes form when molten rock, or magma, makes its way up from the Earth's upper mantle. The upper mantle is about 80 to 150 kilometers below the Earth's surface, where the temperatures are so high that rocks and minerals start to melt. The melting rocks and minerals form magma, and this magma rises up through the solid mantle. Usually an eruption starts because an earthquake breaks the rock at the top of the mantle, and the opening in the rock releases pressure on the gases in the magma. The magma then rises to the surface through a narrow passageway, or what we call the throat of a volcano, and erupts at an opening in the crust, called a vent. Now, when magma flows onto the Earth's surface, we call it lava. An eruption can be dangerous depending on the temperature of the magma and whether it contains a lot of gases. Magma can erupt gently, as lava that flows along the surface of the Earth, or it can erupt explosively, as clouds of ash and rock that rise thousands of meters into the sky.

Narrator: Now complete the steps in your book.

**Narrator: Chapter 2, The Dynamic Earth
Page 33
Note Taking: Using Telegraphic
Language, Step 2**

Patricia Fryer: All right, now let's take a look at some of the basic types of volcanoes. The first kind of volcano is what we call a shield volcano. A shield volcano is usually very, very big. Lava flows out from its vent in gentle eruptions, meaning it flows along the surface of the Earth rather than shooting into the air. The lava cools and becomes hard, forming a broad, sloping shape with a circular base. An example of a shield volcano is Mauna Loa on the Big Island of Hawaii. It's the largest volcano on Earth. Mauna Loa starts on the sea floor and rises to over 9,000 meters high.

Another type of volcano is the composite volcano. They're smaller, though some may be up to 2,500 meters high. These volcanoes have both explosive and gentle eruptions. Often, the volcano will start erupting explosively, and layers of ash and rocks will pile up near the vent. Then the lava flows out and covers these layers of ash, making a cone that has alternating layers of ash and lava. These volcanoes have steeper slopes than shield volcanoes, and they're usually a lot smaller. In general, composites don't erupt as often as shield

volcanoes. A good example is Mt. Fuji in Japan. Another example is Mt. St. Helens, which erupted in 1981.

The smallest volcanoes are cinder cone volcanoes. They're usually less than 200 meters high. They form when lava shoots up into the air and cools quickly. The lava becomes hard in the air and breaks up into small fragments called cinders, which fall to the ground. These cinders pile up around the vent and form a cone with a bowl-shaped crater on the top. Hundreds or thousands of cinder cone volcanoes often form very close to each other. A famous example is Paricutín, in Mexico, in 1943. It grew to nearly 340 meters high in just a few months.

Now, the last type of volcano I'd like to talk about today is the supervolcano. Supervolcanoes are the biggest volcanoes and have the most explosive eruptions. They don't form a cone shape at all; instead, they leave a huge crater in the ground. Eruptions from supervolcanoes are rare, but when they do occur, they cause widespread destruction and can have serious consequences for life on Earth. The largest known supervolcano was Toba. It erupted about 70 to 75 thousand years ago in Indonesia. Some scientists believe it killed at least 60 percent of all people on Earth. Pretty scary!

But most volcanoes give some signs before they actually erupt. These warning signs include earthquakes and ground cracks. Or if drinking water tastes different, it may mean a change in the groundwater, which can also be a sign. And sometimes glaciers at the tops of volcanoes start to melt. Volcanologists, who study active volcanoes, can help in planning for and escaping from dangerous situations.

Narrator: Now complete the steps in your book.

3

Narrator: Chapter 3, Earth's Water Supply
Page 38
Personalizing the Topic, Step 2

Narrator: One.
[*Sound of ducks splashing in water and quacking, along with the gentle lapping of water against the shore.*]

Narrator: Two.
[*Sound of the tide coming in and waves breaking on the shore. Seagulls are calling overhead.*]

Narrator: Three.
[*Steady, loud sound of a large waterfall.*]

Narrator: Four.
[*Sound of the wind blowing strongly in a cold, desolate place and sound of ice creaking.*]

Narrator: Five.
[*Sound of a babbling brook with water running over rocks.*]

Narrator: Now complete the steps in your book.

Narrator: Chapter 3, Earth's Water Supply
Page 40
Listening for Opinions, Step 2

Interviewer: Gina, do you agree that Americans are lucky that we don't have to worry about access to fresh, clean water?

Gina: Oh, yeah. I have traveled to places in the world where you can't drink the water coming out of the tap. In fact, you can't even get it on your toothbrush – you always have to boil it or use water from a bottle. And the first thing I do when I get back to the United States is go pour a glass of water from the tap.

Interviewer: And really enjoy it?

Gina: Yeah, something like that. It just feels so clean. What a luxury, just to turn on the tap.

Interviewer: Even though we can drink tap water in the United States, there are a lot of people who are concerned about pollutants or other contaminants in their drinking water. Is that something you're concerned about?

Gina: Umm . . . Well, sure. I mean, just about everywhere you go in this country, there's been some sort of pollution that affects the drinking water. However, I believe that the people who are in charge of the water supply have done the research, and they know if the water is safe to drink.

Interviewer: You mean you trust that somebody is monitoring your water supply.

Gina: Yes. I mean, I know that there are some places where it may not be safe. But I feel like I'm lucky, because the water where I live seems to be really clean and safe to drink.

Interviewer: So you don't drink bottled water.

Gina: No, no, I'm happy with our tap water. People just like the different tastes of bottled water, and I think that's why they buy it. I mean, I buy it sometimes, but mostly for the convenience of having water bottles to take in the car, and I reuse them most of the time.

Interviewer: It sounds like you're not a big consumer of bottled water, and actually, many people think it hurts the environment when you buy bottled water.

Gina: Right. Because of its packaging. And if we could stop using millions and millions of plastic bottles every day, it would be a relief for our landfills that are quickly reaching capacity.

Narrator: Now complete the steps in your book.

Narrator: Chapter 3, Earth's Water Supply
Page 42
Using a Map to Understand Complex Concepts, Step 3

Interviewer: David and Lara, you lived in Cambodia?

Lara: Yeah, we lived in Cambodia for almost four and a half years. Part of the time we were living in Phnom Penh, the capital. It's a very large, growing city. The other part of the time, we lived in Siem Reap, which is in the countryside.

Interviewer: Well, I want to talk about the water supply. When you were in Cambodia, did you experience problems related to access to safe water?

Lara: Well, when we were in Phnom Penh, the government was working on supplying people with city water. Before that, people would have to buy water from trucks.

Interviewer: So, in the capital city, people didn't have running water in their homes?

Lara: Right.

David: That's right. Many people in the city collect and drink rainwater.

Interviewer: Why can't they have running water?

David: There's no infrastructure, and the people are too poor to pay for that kind of system.

Lara: Once we moved to the country, things were much different.

Interviewer: Better?

Lara: Umm, no.

David: Cambodia has some of the worst problems with water in the world. About 8,000 children die from waterborne illnesses every year there. People drink mostly surface water, which means whatever they can find, like water from a pond. In the countryside, people didn't have enough money to buy wood to boil the water, so they would just drink surface water and get diarrhea.

Interviewer: And that's because the surface water contains . . . ?

David: Feces.

Lara: Feces of cattle, water buffaloes, birds . . . It all drains into the pond, where people wash their cows, and then they drink the water.

Interviewer: So, people don't know that if they drink surface water they'll get sick?

David: Well, they know they should boil the water, and sometimes if they have extra wood, they do boil the water. But in general, they need the wood to cook their food, so they choose not to boil the water. Because they can't buy enough wood.

Interviewer: So, what about you? What did you drink?

David: We tried to bring bottled water with us, and every time we were out, and we had to drink their water, we would ask them to boil it first. But it was still not very nice. It was very thick, sort of a tea color, because it's just what you would take out from a river or a pond.

Interviewer: So this is just something that you dealt with the entire time.

Lara: We did see improvement in one village where we did a project . . .

Interviewer: Ah . . . Can you tell me more about that?

David: Well, basically, everyone in this village had diarrhea almost every week. And then we introduced a ceramic filter, which is like a water pot with a lining that helps kill the bacteria in the water. We were able to give this to almost every family in the village, and the situation completely changed.

Interviewer: People didn't get sick from the water anymore?

David: Right. After a month of using the filter, only four people in the entire village reported having diarrhea. So this is a tremendous change for them. And projects like that are happening throughout the country.

Narrator: Now complete the steps in your book.

**Narrator: Chapter 3, Earth's Water Supply Page 43
Listening for Specific Information, Step 1**

Interviewer: Seónagh, when you lived in Africa, where did you live and how long were you there?

Seónagh: I lived in Cameroon, in West Africa. I lived there for just over a year.

Interviewer: And did you have any trouble getting clean, safe water?

Seónagh: Uh-huh, very much. I was very careful about water, because I had been told you could get all kinds of diseases, so I tried to make sure to boil it or buy bottled water. But then I never had a problem, so I became more relaxed. I sort of just watched what other people did, and I did what they did. That's what made sense to me, because if they weren't getting sick, then I didn't think that I would get sick.

Interviewer: And did you?

Seónagh: No, I didn't. But I can tell you one story about access to water. You know, some parts of Cameroon have really good roads, but in many areas, the roads are really bad. So, the president of Cameroon at that time had a highway going straight to his village and everybody had water.

Interviewer: OK . . .

Seónagh: But I went to another area, which is very difficult to get to because the roads are terrible, and it was heartbreaking because people would travel, um, sometimes ten hours to get water.

Interviewer: From another village?

Seónagh: No. Just from a stream, not even a tap.

Interviewer: Was that because this was a poor community?

Seónagh: Yes. And it's sort of like how people have access to things in the United States. You know, in a poor neighborhood, they may not have electricity, but we assume that everyone has all of these things.

Interviewer: But water is something that you need to survive, it's not a luxury.

Seónagh: Exactly. In Cameroon, I would see women carrying huge buckets of water on their heads, you know? So what I noticed in Africa is that people work very, very hard, and they are able to survive under difficult conditions.

Interviewer: Are people less wasteful of resources like water because of how hard they have to work to get them?

Seónagh: I think people are less wasteful because they have to be. I think that's a natural response to, you know, "This is how much water I have in front of me."

Interviewer: After you returned home from Africa, had you changed?

Seónagh: Yeah, sure. Because seeing someone walk ten miles to get a bucket of water, and she has three small children following her . . . it's just heartbreaking.

Interviewer: I guess it's an image you'll never forget.

Seónagh: Yeah, and so when I turn on my tap, I'm thinking what privilege I have. That has an impact on how I use water, and how I think of water in the world. You know, water's a resource that connects. The ocean touches every continent, right?

Interviewer: Right.

Seónagh: Water comes from the earth and flows across the earth. It's like blood. In some cultures, water is seen as the blood of the earth. I think of it that way. I think of the world as being interconnected and all people being interconnected, all continents, and all of our lives. So, I think of water as sort of a metaphor for that. And I wouldn't want to be wasteful of it.

Narrator: Now complete the steps in your book.

Narrator: Chapter 3, Earth's Water Supply Page 44 Listening for Specific Information, Step 2

Seónagh: Water comes from the earth and flows across the earth. It's like blood. In some cultures, water is seen as the blood of the earth. I think of it that way. I think of the world as being interconnected and all people being interconnected, all continents, and all of our lives. So, I think of water as sort of a metaphor for that. And I wouldn't want to be wasteful of it.

Narrator: Now complete the steps in your book.

Narrator: Chapter 3, Earth's Water Supply
Page 49
Note Taking: Using Symbols and Abbreviations, Step 2

Narrator: One.

Martha McDaniel: Anyone who has ever been to the ocean, or seen a picture of our planet from space, knows that there is plenty of water on Earth. In fact, most of the Earth's surface is covered in water.

Narrator: Two.

Martha McDaniel: However, almost all of that water – 97 percent – is saltwater. That means only 3 percent is freshwater.

Narrator: Three.

Martha McDaniel: Of the 3 percent of water on Earth that is freshwater, almost 75 percent of it is in the form of ice in the coldest regions of our planet. That means that only about 25 percent of the freshwater on Earth is in liquid form.

Narrator: Four.

Martha McDaniel: This small percentage – less than 1 percent of all the water on Earth – provides drinking water for all 6.6 billion people on Earth, as well as all its plants and animals.

Narrator: Five.

Martha McDaniel: Specifically, I would like to focus on the freshwater that can be found on the surface of the planet. This kind of water is called surface water. Freshwater that is beneath the Earth's surface is called groundwater.

Narrator: Now complete the steps in your book.

Narrator: Chapter 3, Earth's Water Supply
Page 51
Note Taking: Using Symbols and Abbreviations, Step 3

Martha McDaniel: Anyone who has ever been to the ocean, or seen a picture of our planet from space, knows that there is plenty of water on Earth. In fact, most of the Earth's surface is covered in water. However,

almost all of that water – 97 percent – is saltwater. That means only 3 percent is freshwater. That doesn't seem like very much freshwater for people to use, and drink, does it? But wait! The amount we can use is even less than that.

Of the 3 percent of water on Earth that is freshwater, almost 75 percent of it is in the form of ice in the coldest regions of our planet. That means that only about 25 percent of the freshwater on Earth is in liquid form. This small percentage – less than 1 percent of all the water on Earth – provides drinking water for all 6.6 billion people on Earth, as well as all its plants and animals. Now *that's* amazing. Today I will talk about this amazing, precious resource: Earth's freshwater supply. Specifically, I would like to focus on the freshwater that can be found on the surface of the planet. This kind of water is called surface water. Freshwater that is beneath the Earth's surface is called groundwater.

Where does freshwater come from? Well, when rain or snow falls from the sky, much of the water sinks into the ground and becomes groundwater. But if the water can't enter the ground, or if the ground is already full of water, then the water stays on the surface. This water starts to move over the surface of the Earth, and as it flows, it cuts a path, or channel, into the land. Over time, the channel becomes deeper, and if the flow of water becomes permanent, it's called a stream. Streams are small, but if they combine with other streams and become bigger, then we can call it a river. Sometimes streams and rivers stop flowing and form a pond or lake. Other times, water keeps flowing across the land until it reaches the ocean.

During the time that freshwater is on the surface of the Earth, in streams and rivers, ponds and lakes, it serves many important functions. Rivers carry nutrients and minerals, and spread them over the land as they flow across the Earth. As a result, most land near rivers is rich and fertile, which means it's very good for growing plants. Many farms are located near rivers for this very reason. When farms are located in drier areas, water has to be carried from natural sources to the farm. This process is called irrigation. Most farmers around the world use surface water for irrigation.

People also use surface water for daily tasks, such as washing dishes and clothes, cleaning and bathing, and so on. Surface water is used in industry, for transportation, and just for playing and enjoyment. But the most important role of surface water is to provide clean water for humans and animals to drink. As I said, without surface water, life on Earth could not exist as it does today.

Narrator: Now complete the steps in your book.

**Narrator: Chapter 3, Earth's Water Supply
Page 53
Note Taking: Using Bullets and Brackets to Organize Your Notes, Step 2**

Martha McDaniel: As you can see, freshwater is critical to life on Earth. Unfortunately, there are many problems threatening Earth's freshwater supply today, and as you might guess, these problems are caused by human beings. As humans build more buildings, roads, and parking lots, the natural environment is lost. Land that once held water is covered with concrete instead. The loss of trees and other plants has an impact on the amount of water, soil, and other nutrients that is able to enter the surface water supply. And these unnatural changes affect the quality of freshwater.

Pollution also affects water quality. Pollution comes from many sources – factories, human waste, pesticides, and fertilizers are just a few examples. Pollution in the air causes acid rain, which falls to Earth and enters the water supply. The trash that people drop on the street may end up in a stream or river. Some water

supplies on Earth can no longer be used, because they have become so polluted.

However, perhaps the biggest threat to our freshwater supply is overuse by humans. The total amount of water on Earth can never increase. In contrast, the number of people is increasing by millions every year. This means millions more people using and drinking water. More people means a need for more food, which means more farming and more water for irrigation. The amount of water used by people is doubling every 20 years, and this is causing problems for many people in the world. According to the World Water Council, more than 1 billion people do not have access to enough clean, safe water.

It is critical that we protect water, which is our most important resource. No human being could live more than a few days without water. Humans must learn to use water more efficiently. For example, new techniques for irrigation could greatly reduce the amount of water that is wasted when watering crops. People can conserve water by making small changes in their daily practices. All countries around the world need to cooperate in order to prevent pollution and manage water resources in order to guarantee access to fresh, clean water.

Narrator: Now complete the steps in your book.

4

**Narrator: CD 2
Chapter 4, Earth's Oceans
Page 57
Sharing Your Opinion, Step 1**

Narrator: Listen to this piece of music by the French composer Claude Debussy. The title is "La Mer," or "The Sea." Debussy wrote this music about the ocean. What kind of ocean does Debussy describe in this music? As you listen, let a picture of the ocean come into your mind. How does this music make you feel? Notice the emotions that you experience. Now, close your eyes and use your imagination.

[*Music plays.*]

Narrator: Now complete the steps in your book.

Narrator: Chapter 4, Earth's Oceans
Page 60
Retelling What You Have Heard, Step 2

Interviewer: I know you love to dive, Edmund. How did you get interested in diving?

Edmund: Well, when I was younger, I thought about being a marine biologist when I grew up. So, I thought, "Maybe I should learn how to dive," and I took a scuba class. But, the instructor said that my swimming was really poor.

Interviewer: So, that must have changed your career plans!

Edmund: Well, like, I could swim, but I was just paddling wrong and going nowhere. So I took a swimming class, and then I got certified in scuba diving later, when I was in high school. And since then, I've been diving consistently.

Interviewer: And with your equipment, your tank, how long can you stay underwater at a time?

Edmund: Let's see . . . eight, nine hours. But the longest I've stayed down is a little over three hours.

Interviewer: And why do you dive? Is it just for fun?

Edmund: Yeah, for fun. I do it to relax, to see things. And I often see something or find something interesting.

Interviewer: Like what?

Edmund: OK, like the last thing I found were these really old bottles. Like I found a hair tonic bottle from the early 1900s. And then a few months ago, I was out and a seahorse swam by, and I got a picture.

Interviewer: So you take photographs underwater, too.

Edmund: Only to show that I saw something. Because if I tell people, "I saw a seahorse," they go, "Yeah, right."

Interviewer: What is it about diving that you like so much? I mean, haven't you gotten bored with it after all these years?

Edmund: Well, I think it's an adventure. It's all these little things that add to your life. It's about having experiences that a lot of people don't have.

Interviewer: And you said you do it to relax?

Edmund: Yeah. To me, it's very peaceful. It's calm, and you can just sit there and look at the fish. It's so tranquil.

Interviewer: It never feels threatening at all?

Edmund: No. Well, when I first started diving by myself, I used to always turn around to look for the shark that would come and get me. It was never there. So I guess you get over it. Although I've had brief moments of fear.

Interviewer: For example?

Edmund: Well . . . a few times a yellow-head eel has come off the bottom and hit me. The first time I felt it hit my hand, and I looked and saw something gray slithering around my chest. And then it swam away.

Interviewer: Wow.

Edmund: And another time, I was swimming along, and I looked up and saw two huge fins, and I started panicking because the fins were bigger than me.

Interviewer: Really!

Edmund: So, I was like [*breathing fast and hard*] and then I told myself, "OK, those are whales, calm down." I was swimming along next to one, and then I guess the whale heard me because it just started rising up and went to the surface. When it did that, I could see that the other one was a baby. It kind of swam off, and I went to the surface to look for them, but they were gone.

Interviewer: When you're down there, do you feel like you're part of the ocean environment?

Edmund: I feel like a visitor, you know? I'm limited because of my equipment. Especially when the currents push you around . . . sometimes I can't get to where I want to go, so I have to go someplace else to look around.

Interviewer: You mean you can't always control where you want to go, and you have to yield to the ocean.

Edmund: Yes, exactly.

Narrator: Now complete the steps in your book.

Narrator: Chapter 4, Earth's Oceans
Page 61
Listening for Main Ideas, Step 2

Interviewer: Hey, Tomoki, let's start with some background questions. When did you first begin surfing and why?

Tomoki: Hmm, I started surfing . . . I believe about five years ago. I'd always been fascinated by the sport, and the reason I finally started was one of my friends gave me a surfboard. So, since I had my own surfboard, I just thought I'd give it a shot.

Interviewer: Did you love surfing right away?

Tomoki: Yeah, right away. Part of the reason is, I've always loved the ocean. When I was a child, I remember that every summer I spent all my time at the beach, playing in the water. So, yeah, when I tried surfing, I couldn't even sit or stand up on the board, but I liked it immediately.

Interviewer: So, it's pretty hard to stand up the first time?

Tomoki: It's challenging. It's not something you can do right away. You need to practice, and as you practice, you can feel your own progress.

Interviewer: Hmm. What conditions are best for surfing?

Tomoki: Well, I think physically, you need to be fit, and that means you need to be able to paddle. And in order to stand up on the board, you need to have good balance and coordination. That's the physical part. And the best conditions for surfing? Well, you need to have waves.

Interviewer: Obviously! What about the size of the wave?

Tomoki: It depends on what you like. I like bigger waves, but I don't want to surf waves that are too big. People describe waves as waist-high or shoulder-high or head-high. I like maybe shoulder-high to a little bit over head-high. I like that size.

Interviewer: And, what about wind? Is wind good for surfing or not?

Tomoki: Not too good. Many surfers hope that there's no wind.

Interviewer: But doesn't the wind bring the waves?

Tomoki: Yeah, but if there's too much wind, the surface of the ocean is not that clean. We say that the surface is choppy or clean. Surfers always want to have a clean surface.

Interviewer: Now, could you describe to a nonsurfer what it feels like to surf?

Tomoki: Well, it feels like you're sliding over the wave, but the wave is always moving, everything is moving together. It's very dynamic, meaning the situation is always changing.

Interviewer: OK, I can imagine that.

Tomoki: It feels like you're flying through the water. And the shape of the wave is so beautiful. Sometimes, you can see inside the ocean – you can actually look inside the curve of the wave and see fish and the ocean floor. How do you feel? It just feels good.

Interviewer: Do you feel that you're controlling the movement of your surfboard, or do you have to go where the wave takes you?

Tomoki: Hmm . . . Both. You really feel the power of nature, the power of the waves in your whole body. The waves are moving your entire body from point A to point B. You need that power, but you also need to be able to control the movement. So, maybe that's why it's so fascinating, because you can't just do it by yourself. That's why surfing is so unique.

Narrator: Now complete the steps in your book.

Narrator: Chapter 4, Earth's Oceans
Page 61
Thinking Critically About the Topic, Step 2

Narrator: Listen to the last part of the interview with Edmund.

Interviewer: When you're down there, do you feel like you're part of the ocean environment?

Edmund: I feel like a visitor, you know? I'm limited because of my equipment. Especially when the currents push you around . . . sometimes I can't get to where I want to go, so I have to go someplace else to look around.

Interviewer: You mean you can't always control where you want to go, and you have to yield to the ocean.

Edmund: Yes, exactly.

Narrator: Listen to the last part of the interview with Tomoki.

Interviewer: Do you feel that you're controlling the movement of your surfboard, or do you have to go where the wave takes you?

Tomoki: Hmm . . . Both. You really feel the power of nature, the power of the waves in your whole body. The waves are moving your entire body from point A to point B. You need that power, but you also need to be able to control the movement. So, maybe that's why it's so fascinating, because you can't just do it by yourself. That's why surfing is so unique.

Narrator: Now complete the steps in your book.

Narrator: Chapter 4, Earth's Oceans
Page 66
Note Taking: Listening for Signal Words, Step 3

Narrator: One.

Geoff Haywood: Of course, all of our oceans are also connected to many smaller seas, like the Mediterranean, the Aegean, the China Sea, and so on.

Narrator: Two.

Geoff Haywood: As you know, warm water is less dense than cold water, so this warmer water stays at the surface of the ocean while the colder water sinks.

Narrator: Three.

Geoff Haywood: As I just said, the surface layer is relatively warm, with an average temperature of 15 degrees Celsius.

Narrator: Four.

Geoff Haywood: And because sunlight quickly fades below the sunlit zone, no plants can grow. Consequently, most of the animals living in the middle layer have to swim up to the surface layer to find food.

Narrator: Five.

Geoff Haywood: The animals that live here have special adaptations to live in these conditions. For example, many fish in the midnight zone do not have eyes.

Narrator: Six.

Geoff Haywood: Incidentally, the pressure at the bottom of the ocean is very, very high. Before I finish this lecture, let me talk a little about water pressure.

Narrator: Seven.

Geoff Haywood: Now, once we go in the ocean, the water – because it is much denser than air – puts far greater pressure on us. In fact, for every 10 meters that we go down in the ocean, we increase that pressure on us by one more kilogram per square centimeter.

Narrator: Now complete the steps in your book.

Narrator: Chapter 4, Earth's Oceans
Page 68
Note Taking: Using Handouts to Help You Take Notes, Step 2

Geoff Haywood: The topic of our lecture today is Earth's oceans. The percentage of our planet that is covered by ocean water is actually very high. Eighty percent of the Southern Hemisphere is ocean; 61 percent of the Northern Hemisphere is also ocean, resulting in a total average of 71 percent of the planet's surface covered in ocean. We can think of it as a world ocean, which is divided into four main ocean basins. These are the Atlantic Ocean, which stretches between Europe and the American continent; the Pacific Ocean, which is the largest and deepest ocean, and which stretches between the American continent and Asia; and the Indian Ocean, which surrounds India. In the northern polar regions of our planet, we also have the Arctic Ocean, which is the smallest and shallowest ocean. Some people argue that there is one more ocean, called the Southern Ocean, which surrounds the Antarctic continent. Of course, all of our oceans are also connected to many smaller seas, like the Mediterranean, the Aegean, the China Sea, and so on. As a result of this, all oceans and seas are connected, and water is constantly moving and mixing from one ocean to the other and from one sea to the other. This is why we can think of all of our planet's oceans and seas as one world ocean.

Narrator: Now complete the steps in your book.

Narrator: Chapter 4, Earth's Oceans
   Page 70
   Note Taking: Using Handouts to Help You Take Notes, Step 1

Geoff Haywood: Earth's oceans are extremely deep, averaging 3,800 meters from the surface down to the ocean floor. As one goes down from the surface, one finds a very interesting feature: the ocean has a layered structure. This is because seawater has different densities. Let's look at each of the three main layers, one by one.

The first layer – called the surface layer – is the top 100 to 200 meters of the ocean. This layer is sometimes called the "sunlit zone" because the sun penetrates this layer. Therefore, the seawater here has been heated by the sun. As you know, warm water is less dense than cold water, so this

warmer water stays at the surface of the ocean while the colder water sinks. Most of the ocean's fish and other marine life live in the surface layer, where they can find a lot of algae and other plants to eat.

After the first 200 meters or so of the ocean, the surface layer ends and the middle layer begins. The middle ocean layer goes down to about 1,000 meters in depth. The most notable feature here is a rapid drop in temperature. As I just said, the surface layer is relatively warm, with an average temperature of 15 degrees Celsius. By contrast, in the middle layer, water quickly becomes colder with every meter of depth. By 1,000 meters, the average temperature of the ocean water is only 4 degrees Celsius. And because sunlight quickly fades below the sunlit zone, no plants can grow. Consequently, most of the animals living in the middle layer have to swim up to the surface layer to find food.

Below the middle layer of the ocean, there is the bottom layer, which is all the cold, dense water below 1,000 meters in depth. As you can imagine, since no sunlight can penetrate this deep, the water here is pitch black. As a result, this layer is sometimes called the "midnight zone." It has very cold, almost freezing, temperatures. The animals that live here have special adaptations to live in these conditions. For example, many fish in the midnight zone do not have eyes. Some give off their own light. Much of the ocean's bottom layer hasn't been studied yet, so scientists still don't know a lot about this deep environment.

Narrator: Now complete the steps in your book.

Narrator: Chapter 4, Earth's Oceans
   Page 71
   Note Taking: Using Handouts to Help You Take Notes, Step 1

Geoff Haywood: Incidentally, the pressure at the bottom of the ocean is very, very high. Before I finish this lecture, let me talk a little about water pressure. We on Earth live at the bottom of an ocean of air. In other words, our atmosphere can be thought of as an ocean, and we are living at the bottom of it. The air that we breathe right now is at a pressure of about 1 kilogram per square centimeter. You might not realize this because of course the air inside you is pushing out at the same pressure as the air outside is pushing in. But as I said, the air that we are breathing is under pressure. Now, once we go in the ocean, the water – because it is much denser than air – puts far greater pressure on us. In fact, for every 10 meters that we go down in the ocean, we increase that pressure on us by one more kilogram per square centimeter. This is what we call one atmosphere of pressure. At the bottom of the ocean, the pressure can be as high as 600 atmospheres, or 600 kilograms per square centimeter.

So let's just review very quickly what we talked about today. We have four main oceans: the Atlantic, the Pacific, the Indian Ocean, and the Arctic Ocean. There are many seas. Oceans are also connected to seas, and as a result, we can say that all the bodies of saltwater on our planet are interconnected. The oceans are deep and have a layered structure: there's a surface layer, a middle layer, and a bottom layer. Finally, pressure increases with depth, so that as we go down into the ocean every 10 meters, the pressure increases by one atmosphere, or 1 kilogram per square centimeter. There is much, much more to learn about the ocean. It's the last unexplored region on Earth.

Narrator: Now complete the steps in your book.

Narrator: Chapter 4, Earth's Oceans
Page 72
Note Taking: Focusing on the Conclusion, Step 1

Geoff Haywood: So let's just review very quickly what we talked about today. We have four

main oceans: the Atlantic, the Pacific, the Indian Ocean, and the Arctic Ocean. There are many seas. Oceans are also connected to seas, and as a result, we can say that all the bodies of saltwater on our planet are interconnected. The oceans are deep and have a layered structure: there's a surface layer, a middle layer, and a bottom layer. Finally, pressure increases with depth, so that as we go down into the ocean every 10 meters, the pressure increases by one atmosphere, or 1 kilogram per square centimeter. There is much, much more to learn about the ocean. It's the last unexplored region on Earth.

Narrator: Now complete the steps in your book.

Narrator: Chapter 5, Earth's Atmosphere
Page 75
Listening for Background Noise, Step 2

Narrator: Listen. Where is the person in picture A?
[*Sounds of a rain forest – tropical birds and insects. Someone sounds hot and uncomfortable.*]

Narrator: Listen. Where is the person in picture B?
[*Sounds of the countryside – a gentle breeze and birds twittering. Someone is sniffling and sneezing.*]

Narrator: Listen. Where is the person in picture C?
[*Sounds of a strong wind whistling and howling. Someone is having trouble breathing.*]

Narrator: Listen. Where is the person in picture D?
[*Sounds of the city – honking horns and busy traffic. Someone is coughing.*]

Narrator: Now complete the steps in your book.

Narrator: Listen. Why is the person in each picture having problems? Picture A.

Man: It's so hot here . . . and humid, too. I'm going to need to take a shower after our hike.

Narrator: Picture B.

Woman: I knew I should have stayed at home. There is so much pollen in the air today. And my allergies are just killing me.

Narrator: Picture C.

Man: Oh, it's difficult to breathe up here. The air is so thin. I can't get enough oxygen in my lungs.

Narrator: Picture D.

Man: Oh, boy, the traffic's bad today. And it's so smoggy. I hope I don't get sick.

Narrator: Now complete the steps in your book.

Narrator: **Chapter 5, Earth's Atmosphere**
   Page 78
   Listening for Specific Information, Step 2

Interviewer: Jeff, as director of an environmental group, you're concerned with air quality and its effects on people and nature, is that right?

Jeff: Yes, that's right.

Interviewer: What are some factors that affect air quality?

Jeff: Well, there are a number of factors that affect air quality: pollutants in the air, from either human activity or from natural sources . . .

Narrator: Now complete the steps in your book.

Narrator: **Chapter 5, Earth's Atmosphere**
   Page 78
   Listening for Specific Information, Step 3

Interviewer: Jeff, as director of an environmental group, you're concerned with air quality and its effects on people and nature, is that right?

Jeff: Yes, that's right.

Interviewer: What are some factors that affect air quality?

Jeff: Well, there are a number of factors that affect air quality: pollutants in the air, from either human activity or from natural sources . . .

Interviewer: Can you give some examples?

Jeff: Well, the most common man-made pollution that you see comes from burning fossil fuels. So burning of oil or natural gas or coal, by factories, power plants . . .

Interviewer: And cars, right? I think that's the example that most people are familiar with.

Jeff: Cars create a number of pollutants in the air. The most obvious is particulate matter, which is tiny pieces of matter that are small enough to float in the air.

Interviewer: Can you see particulate matter in the air?

Jeff: Well, you can when there's enough of it. In fact, if you look at a factory, sometimes you can see a dark cloud coming out. That's the particulate matter. Some of it settles on the ground. If you're in a really industrial area, you might see a coating on cars or on the ground. But some of it is so small – in fact, they measure this in microns, or millionths of a meter – very small particles.

Interviewer: So people don't notice when they breathe them in?

Jeff: Usually not. But even though we can't feel them, they can cause damage to our lungs.

Interviewer: Can you give me some examples of natural sources of particulate matter?

Jeff: Natural sources . . . well, one is a wildfire that starts naturally from a lightning strike or something like that. When a wildfire burns, it sends a lot of particulate matter in the air. Or, a windstorm, like in the desert, blows pieces of soil into the air. These are a couple of examples of natural sources.

Narrator: Now complete the steps in your book.

Narrator: Chapter 5, Earth's Atmosphere
Page 79
Listening for Specific Information, Step 1

Interviewer: Shari, you grew up in Los Angeles. Tell me about the air quality there.

Shari: Well, it can be bad, especially in the summertime. There were mountains near where I was living, but you couldn't even see the mountains at certain times of the year.

Interviewer: What did it actually look like, when it was bad like that?

Shari: It looked hazy . . . it was like fog, but it was brown like smoke, and that's why they call it "smog" – smoke and fog mixed together. So, it just looks hazy, but it's brown.

Interviewer: And did you feel like it was affecting you physically?

Shari: Sure. Um, when I was younger, I got really bad headaches when there was a lot of smog. Sometimes the headaches were so bad, I could hardly think. And it was difficult to breathe.

Interviewer: That's not good.

Shari: Yeah. They used to have smog level advisories during the weather report, and I think it was between zero and five. Five was dangerous, and zero was completely clear. If it was over three or four, there were advisories. And in school, if it was above three or four when we went to PE, we wouldn't even be allowed to exercise outside.

Interviewer: So this advisory tells you how much smog is in the air.

Shari: Right, the amount of pollution. And so when it reached a certain level, the city decided that it was dangerous to exercise outdoors, and we'd have indoor activities during PE.

Narrator: Now complete the steps in your book.

Narrator: Chapter 5, Earth's Atmosphere
Page 79
Listening for Specific Information, Step 2

Shari: They used to have smog level advisories during the weather report, and I think it was between zero and five. Five was dangerous, and zero was completely clear. If it was over three or four, there were advisories. And in school, if it was above three or four when we went to PE, we wouldn't even be allowed to exercise outside.

Narrator: Now complete the steps in your book.

Narrator: Chapter 5, Earth's Atmosphere
Page 81
Answering Multiple Choice Questions, Step 2

Interviewer: Kelley, you've lived in a humid environment, and Michael, you've lived in a very dry environment. Now, I know that you're a very athletic person, Kelley. What sports do you like?

Kelley: Well, I like surfing, hiking, running, volleyball, basketball, and I especially love cycling.

Interviewer: Could you tell me how the air affects you as an athlete in a humid environment?

Kelley: I think the most important factor for athletes is humidity. So if there's more moisture in the air, it can be very uncomfortable.

Interviewer: Why is that?

Kelley: Because when you're playing sports, your body makes a lot of heat. You need to get rid of some of that heat by sweating.

Interviewer: I see. So sweating takes the heat out of our bodies. But how is that related to humidity?

Kelley: Well, if it's humid, there's already a lot of water in the air, so the sweat stays on your skin and you still feel hot. Otherwise, the sweat would evaporate and cool your skin.

Interviewer: So when it's humid, it's harder to cool your body down?

Kelley: Right. And you may feel more tired.

Interviewer: Michael, you were living in California, right?

Michael: Yeah, down in the desert near Mexico. They only get 2 to 3 inches of rain in a year, so it's very, very dry.

Interviewer: And hot?

Michael: Yep, it's one of the hottest places in the world, actually. In the summertime, the average high temperature is about 112 degrees Fahrenheit. And one day when I was there, it reached 126 degrees. It was so dry that the wind blew up a dust storm.

Interviewer: What was that like?

Michael: Well, it was like fog – you could barely see. We got out of our car, and the wind was blowing the sand all around us, just like the movies. It was so hot, it was unbearable. So we spent maybe a minute outside the car, and then we said, "This is crazy. Let's get out of here!"

Interviewer: Did living in the desert affect you physically?

Michael: It was difficult to get used to the strong heat. So I'd have to drink a lot to make sure I didn't get dehydrated. In fact, I probably drank, oh, a half-gallon to a gallon of sports drinks a day.

Interviewer: How was the air quality?

Michael: Most of the time, the air was very clean. But it did dry you out. My lips and skin were dry all the time, and when it was really hot and dry, you had to be careful not to exercise too much. It would almost hurt your lungs. You'd want to wait until it cooled down a bit in the evening.

Narrator: Now complete the steps in your book.

Narrator: Chapter 5, Earth's Atmosphere
Page 85
Note Taking: Identifying Key Vocabulary in the Lecture, Steps 1 and 2

Narrator: One.

Kyo Narita: Most of the water in the air is in the form of gas. When water changes from a liquid to a gas, it's called water vapor.

Narrator: Two.

Kyo Narita: All air has some water vapor, but there can be big differences in how much. The amount of water vapor in the air – that is, the humidity level – is something I know you're all familiar with.

Narrator: Three.

Kyo Narita: Have you ever thought about the idea of solids in the air? The term *particulate matter* is defined as any tiny pieces of solids that are floating in the air.

Narrator: Four.

Kyo Narita: Flowers, trees, plants – they release pollen, or a powder made by flowers, and other natural matter.

Narrator: Five.

Kyo Narita: Humans also add particulate matter to the air. As a result, there are some substances in the air that shouldn't be there, or there's too much of certain substances, and this is what we know as pollution.

Narrator: Now complete the steps in your book.

Narrator: Chapter 5, Earth's Atmosphere
Page 87
Note Taking: Organizing Your Notes in an Outline, Step 2

Kyo Narita: Take a deep breath. Have you ever thought about what you breathe in, every time you take a breath? We can't see it, we can't feel it, but air is all around us. We often think that air is empty. But air actually contains many different things. Today I'd like to talk about what's in the air out there.

You probably know that the air around you contains a lot of different gases. Nitrogen and oxygen, for example, are the two main gases that air is composed of. Nitrogen makes up 78 percent and oxygen makes up 21 percent of the air we breathe. But there are also about ten other gases that can be found in small amounts. And even though we can't see or smell or taste these gases, we couldn't live without them.

There's a lot of water in the air we breathe. Most of the water in the air is in the form of gas. When water changes from a liquid to a gas, it's called water vapor. All air has some water vapor, but there can be big differences in how much. The amount of water vapor in the air – that is, the humidity level – is something I know you're all familiar with. If you hear on the news that today's humidity is 80 percent, that means there's a lot of water vapor in the air, and you'll probably feel uncomfortable. But if you hear that today's humidity is 50 percent, that means there's a lot less water in the air. Fifty percent is comfortable for most people. Deserts and other arid places can have a humidity level of only 10 percent – not much water at all.

What do these percentages mean? Does 50 percent humidity mean that the air is half full of water? Of course not! Air can only hold a certain amount of water – a total possible amount of water. The percentage of humidity refers to how much of this total possible amount is in the air. So 50 percent humidity means that the air contains half of the total amount of water it can hold.

Before we move on, let's talk about how water vapor gets into the air. The most obvious source is precipitation, which can change from liquid to vapor as it falls from the clouds. But water vapor can also enter the air from sources on Earth: from oceans and rivers, from trees and plants, and even from the ground.

Narrator: Now complete the steps in your book.

**Narrator: Chapter 5, Earth's Atmosphere
Page 89
Note Taking: Organizing Your Notes in a Chart, Step 2**

Kyo Narita: So far, we've talked about gases and water vapor in the air. Have you ever thought about the idea of solids in the air? The term *particulate matter* is defined as any tiny pieces of solids that are floating in the air. In other words, these are pieces of matter that are so small that they're carried in the air, and they're too light to fall to the ground. There are many different kinds of particulate matter; some are found in the air naturally, and others are man-made, that is, they're the result of human activity. I'd like to talk about a couple different types of particulate matter, first those that occur naturally.

When a volcano erupts, it shoots smoke and ash into the air. In the same way, a forest fire fills up the air with smoke and soot. When the ocean waves crash against the shore, salt and sand escape. Flowers, trees, plants – they release pollen, or a powder made by flowers, and other natural matter. Have you ever walked through a field and then started sneezing? That might be pollen in the air entering your nose. Dirt and dust may be picked up by the wind, then fly into our eyes and make them red and itchy. And finally, there are naturally occurring viruses, molds, even bacteria, that are found in the air.

Humans also add particulate matter to the air. As a result, there are some substances in the air that shouldn't be there, or there's too much of certain substances, and this is what we know as pollution. When humans burn wood for cooking and heating, or they burn bushes or trees, they add particulate matter to the air. When humans remove trees and take water from the land, it's easier for dirt and dust to be picked up and carried in the air. But the activity that creates the most pollution is the burning of coal and other fossil fuels. This means every time we use fuel to power a factory or run a car, particulate matter is added to the air we breathe.

When we breathe those particles in, they can hurt our eyes, our throat, our nose, or cause more serious health problems. Let me just remind you: The next time you look around at all that "empty" air, there really is a lot in there.

Narrator: Now complete the steps in your book.

6

**Narrator: Chapter 6, Weather and Climate
Page 92
Listening for Specific Information,
Step 2**

Narrator: One.
Male forecaster: It's going to be a beautiful day today! We're looking at a clear sky, no clouds, and warm temperatures. Be sure to get outside and enjoy the weather!

Narrator: Two.
Female forecaster: You may want to leave work early this afternoon, folks. It's already dark and cloudy, and the wind is strong. The thunderstorm will be here in about an hour. Be careful driving!

Narrator: Three.
Male forecaster: It's getting colder and colder. The rain that started earlier this morning has changed to snow, and it's falling pretty hard. It looks like temperatures are going to be below freezing tonight, so be prepared for a lot of snow tomorrow morning.

Narrator: Four.
Female forecaster: The good news is, the heavy showers have ended. The bad news is, we're still going to have a lot of drizzle and fog today. But it's definitely better than yesterday.

Narrator: Now complete the steps in your book.

**Narrator: Chapter 6, Weather and Climate
Page 94
Listening for Specific Information,
Step 2**

Interviewer: Sara, tell me a little bit about yourself.
Sara: OK. Well, originally I'm from Portugal, but right now I'm a graduate student here in the U.S. I'm in the first year of my Ph.D. in meteorology.
Interviewer: Could you explain what meteorology is?
Sara: Well, meteorology is a way of describing and trying to understand what happens in the atmosphere.
Interviewer: How did you become interested in it?
Sara: It's funny, when I was a teenager, I couldn't decide what I wanted to be. My father always told me science is a great field. He said, "Science is very good. Scientists can do many things." I guess I was influenced by him because I chose science as my major.
Interviewer: So your father influenced your decision.
Sara: Yes. But I've always had a fascination with the sky. When I was young, I would stare at the sky, looking at the clouds and watching them pass. I wanted to know why one cloud is different from another one. And one day when I was around 17 years old, I told my mother, "Why don't I study meteorology? I like the sky!"
Interviewer: Are you happy with your choice?
Sara: Yes, very happy. Our atmosphere is so important. People don't realize – I think because we can't see air, we think the air is nothing. But that's not true. Think of it this way: The Earth is like a big aquarium, we're just like fish, and our atmosphere is just like water. Fish need water to survive and we need air. Without the atmosphere, all human beings on Earth would die.

Narrator: Now complete the steps in your book.

Narrator: Chapter 6, Weather and Climate
Page 94
Listening for Specific Information,
Step 3

Sara: Our atmosphere is so important. People don't realize – I think because we can't see air, we think the air is nothing. But that's not true. Think of it this way: The Earth is like a big aquarium, we're just like fish, and our atmosphere is just like water. Fish need water to survive and we need air. Without the atmosphere, all human beings on Earth would die.

Narrator: Now complete the steps in your book.

Narrator: Chapter 6, Weather and Climate
Page 95
Predicting the Content, Step 1

Narrator: One.
Interviewer: Dorothy, tell us about your experience.
Dorothy: Well, I was in a blizzard last October. It really was a freak storm. I mean, generally we don't get that kind of snow in New York in October.

Narrator: Two.
Interviewer: Yukiya, what kind of severe weather did you experience?
Yukiya: In my case, I was caught in a flood about two years ago.

Narrator: Three.
Interviewer: Evylynn, you were also in a dangerous situation.
Evylynn: That's right. When I was 16, Hurricane Iniki struck my hometown on the island of Kauai.

Narrator: Now complete the steps in your book.

Narrator: Chapter 6, Weather and Climate
Page 96
Predicting the Content, Step 3

Interviewer: You've all had experiences with severe weather. Dorothy, tell us about your experience.

Dorothy: Well, I was in a blizzard last October. It really was a freak storm. I mean, generally we don't get that kind of snow in New York in October. The snow started falling on a Thursday, and it was falling very fast, and by Friday morning we had about two feet of it.
Interviewer: Two feet of snow!
Dorothy: The worst part was that it was very heavy, wet snow. And the weight of the snow brought down a lot of tree limbs. And the tree limbs brought down the power lines, and so many people were left without electricity. The power was off for two weeks – in some places even longer.
Interviewer: Did you lose power in your home?
Dorothy: Yes, but we were lucky. The power came back on after four days. Many other people were without power for two weeks or more. The other sad part was, the area where the storm hit lost 50 percent of its trees, so really, it was terrible.
Interviewer: Yukiya, what kind of severe weather did you experience?
Yukiya: In my case, I was caught in a flood about two years ago.
Interviewer: What do you remember about it?
Yukiya: I remember I was at school, studying, and at that time I was stressed out about my homework, you know? And it was raining really hard, but I didn't pay much attention to it. Then all of a sudden the lights went out. So I went outside, and when I opened the door, I saw all this water pouring into the parking lot!
Interviewer: Coming toward you?
Yukiya: Well, it was flooding into the parking lot. It looked like a pool. But I couldn't go anywhere else, so I had to go through the water, and it came up to my knees, and then up to my waist. I actually saw one car floating!
Interviewer: Was it still raining?
Yukiya: It was raining really hard. And all around me there was water and mud and tree branches, and all kinds of debris. It was crazy.
Interviewer: Were you scared?

Yukiya: Yes, but at the same time, I was kind of excited. I'd never seen anything like that before. I was like, "This is definitely going to be on the news!" I was relieved to finally get home, around midnight. I was fine, just, you know . . . I was soaking wet!

Interviewer: Evylynn, you were also in a dangerous situation.

Evylynn: That's right. When I was 16, Hurricane Iniki struck my hometown on the island of Kauai.

Interviewer: Hurricane Iniki was a Category 4 hurricane. Wasn't it the most powerful hurricane ever to hit Hawaii?

Evylynn: Yes, and Kauai was right in the center of it. I remember when the hurricane hit – it was amazing. Houses right across the street from me were torn apart. Trees were uprooted and thrown down the street. Trees and lamp posts were flying everywhere.

Interviewer: Scary.

Evylynn: Yes, it was scary, but I also thought it was kind of fun. I guess that sounds strange, but I was pretty young at the time, so it was exciting. Of course I was worried about the families in the houses that were destroyed.

Interviewer: Was your house damaged?

Evylynn: Not too badly. There was a lot of flooding and water damage. Afterwards, the whole island didn't have power for a couple of months. But you know, the people in my community came together in a lot of ways. And I know if there's ever a warning about a natural disaster, I need to take it seriously. Once you experience something like that, you remember it for the rest of your life.

Narrator: Now complete the steps in your book.

**Narrator: Chapter 6, Weather and Climate
Page 96
Listening for Opinions, Step 1**

Interviewer: I'd like to ask you all about global warming. Sara, you're a meteorologist. Do you think global warming is affecting our weather on Earth?

Sara: Well, my opinion is, global warming is really happening, and everybody knows that. And everybody knows that human beings are a little bit responsible for it. But there are some changes that I think are natural . . . changes that would probably happen even without people.

Interviewer: So, global warming is not affecting our weather?

Sara: I don't know. With science, until you have the right answer, you can't say for sure. I can't say for sure if it's affecting our weather or not.

Interviewer: Dorothy, do you think global warming is affecting our weather?

Dorothy: I do. Just look at the weather in different areas. Hurricanes are becoming stronger and more severe. I don't think it's just the natural cycle of things. I can see how the weather patterns have changed just in my hometown. The winters used to be more severe, and now they're warmer and there isn't as much snow.

Interviewer: Yukiya?

Yukiya: I agree with Dorothy. I'm not a scientist or anything, but I've heard that global warming is melting the ice and the glaciers in Antarctica, and the water level of our oceans is going up, and that's what causes the hurricanes. I'm sure global warming plays some role.

Interviewer: Evylynn?

Evylynn: I agree. I think global warming is making the weather worse, and there's more risk of dangerous storms. Obviously because humans are changing the Earth, that's causing the weather to change. We need to start doing something soon to protect our environment, or it's all going to be gone.

Narrator: Now complete the steps in your book.

Narrator: Chapter 6, Weather and Climate
Page 100
Note Taking: Listening for Numerical Information, Step 2

Narrator: One.

Fred Mackenzie: Since the beginning of the planet, about 4.6 billion years ago, there has been a mixture of gases surrounding the Earth.

Narrator: Two.

Fred Mackenzie: Energy from the sun enters our atmosphere at its top. This energy, or radiation, is very, very strong. About 45 percent of it reaches the Earth's surface, where it's absorbed by the oceans, the land, and the forests.

Narrator: Three.

Fred Mackenzie: This has led to a heating of the Earth's surface over the past 100 to 150 years, and the average temperature has risen by 1 degree centigrade.

Narrator: Four.

Fred Mackenzie: Today I'd like to focus on two effects of global warming. The first is an increase in sea level. The sea level has risen over the past 100 years, between about 15 and 25 centimeters.

Narrator: Five.

Fred Mackenzie: Unless we change the way we do things today – that is, relying on fossil fuels for 90 percent of our global energy resources – it's likely that the amount of greenhouse gases will continue to increase and temperatures will continue to rise.

Narrator: Now complete the steps in your book.

Narrator: Chapter 6, Weather and Climate
Page 101
Note Taking: Copying a Lecturer's Illustrations, Step 2

Fred Mackenzie: Well, before I talk about global warming, I'm going to give you some background about Earth's atmosphere, or the gases around the planet. Since the beginning of the planet, about 4.6 billion years ago, there has been a mixture of gases surrounding the Earth. Some of these gases, like carbon dioxide, methane, nitrous oxide, and ozone, are called greenhouse gases. We call them greenhouse gases because they create a "greenhouse effect." That is, they cause the lower atmosphere to warm up, because they absorb heat radiation.

Let's look at the greenhouse effect, to get a better idea of what these greenhouse gases do. Energy from the sun enters our atmosphere at its top. This energy, or radiation, is very, very strong. About 45 percent of it reaches the Earth's surface, where it's absorbed by the oceans, the land, and the forests. Then, this energy is radiated back to space from the Earth's surface. The energy coming from Earth is captured by the greenhouse gases in the atmosphere. In other words, the energy does not return back into space, but instead is kept inside the Earth's atmosphere. This process warms the Earth's surface and has maintained a pleasant climate on our planet almost since its beginning. This is the natural greenhouse effect.

Now, we've always had greenhouse gases in our atmosphere, and we've always had a natural greenhouse effect on this planet. But what has happened in the past century or so is that human activities have added gases to the atmosphere. As a result, the greenhouse effect has increased. With more greenhouse gases in the atmosphere, more energy from the Earth is absorbed. This has led to a heating of the Earth's surface over the past 100 to 150 years, and the average temperature has risen by 1 degree centigrade. While there has been a lot of debate, I think people have realized that the problem of global warming is due to the increased greenhouse effect.

Narrator: Now complete the steps in your book.

Narrator: Chapter 6, Weather and Climate
Page 103
Note Taking: Listening for Cause and Effect, Step 2

Fred Mackenzie: What are the consequences of this increase in Earth's temperature? There are many. Today I'd like to focus on two effects of global warming. The first is an increase in sea level. The sea level has risen over the past 100 years, between about 15 and 25 centimeters. It's rising and will continue to rise in the future. Some of this rise is due to the heating of the ocean surface: As the oceans warm, they expand and the sea level rises. Another cause is that mountain glaciers and snow cover are melting. The melt water is entering the ocean and resulting in a rise in sea level. Some scientists also believe that the Greenland ice cap is melting.

A second consequence of global warming is changes in the weather itself. As Earth's temperatures continue to rise, some areas of the world will become wetter, and some will become drier. Already, many countries around the world are experiencing more and longer periods of drought. In fact, the amount of land affected by drought has doubled since the 1970s. Another example of weather change is an increase in severe storm activity. Some scientists believe that if the warming continues, we'll have more hurricanes. Hurricanes develop over warm oceans, and so the rise in ocean temperatures may cause more and perhaps stronger hurricanes.

There are many other consequences of global warming, including melting of the polar ice caps, extinction of some plant and animal species, and a decline in air quality.

It's difficult to predict the future. Unless we change the way we do things today – that is, relying on fossil fuels for 90 percent of our global energy resources – it's likely that the amount of greenhouse gases will continue to increase and temperatures will continue to rise. A prediction for the 21st century is that we're likely to see temperatures about 3 degrees centigrade higher than they are now. Sea levels are likely to be higher, about 60 centimeters above their current level.

So, global warming is a real problem for all of us. And I think how we deal with it is not simply a scientific or political issue, it's also an ethical issue, particularly how we deal with it as individuals.

Narrator: Now complete the steps in your book.

7

Narrator: CD 3
Chapter 7, Life on Earth
Page 108
Listening for Specific Information, Step 4

Narrator: One.
Man: Trees are the biggest plants in the world. The largest species of tree on Earth is the giant sequoia. These trees grow naturally in California. They can grow to more than 100 meters tall and 17 meters wide.

Narrator: Two.
Woman: The blue whale is the largest animal in the world. Many scientists think that there has been no animal in the history of Earth that was larger than the blue whale. A blue whale can grow up to 33 meters long and weigh as much as 150 tons. Its heart is the same size as a small car. Blue whales live in the deepest waters of all the world's oceans.

Narrator: Three.
Man: Many people think that bamboo is a kind of tree, but it is actually a kind of grass. Bamboo is the fastest-growing plant on Earth – it can grow 4 centimeters in just one hour! Bamboo can be found in many different climates, from cold mountains to hot, tropical jungles.

Narrator: Four.
Woman: The platypus is so unusual-looking that the scientists who first heard about

it did not think it was a real animal. The platypus lives only in Australia. It looks like a duck, but it has a wide, flat tail. It lives on land but is a very good swimmer. One of the most interesting facts about the platypus is that it is one of the few mammals that lays eggs instead of giving birth to babies.

Narrator: Five.

Man: The Venus flytrap is one of Earth's rare carnivorous plants; in other words, it is a plant that eats meat. The Venus flytrap snaps shut when an insect or small animal touches its leaves; then it eats the insect. This plant's natural habitat is in the southern United States, but it now grows all over the world. It is also a popular houseplant.

Narrator: Six.

Woman: Ninety-five percent of all animals on Earth are insects, and almost half of all insects are beetles. Scientists have already found 350,000 species of beetles. They live everywhere on Earth, except for the ocean and polar regions. The beetle pictured here is the Goliath beetle, the largest and heaviest of all insects.

Narrator: Now complete the steps in your book.

Narrator: Chapter 7, Life on Earth
Page 111
Listening for Specific Information,
Step 2

Interviewer: Frank, you're an avid gardener, right? How did you get started?

Frank: Well, let me take you back a long, long time. I was a kid in the '30s and '40s, and everybody had gardens, because times were tough. So, wherever you found a little space, you'd plant some radishes or some tomatoes, or something like that. And so, because I grew up in that situation, I was always interested in growing things. These days, I enjoy collecting and growing local native plants.

Interviewer: What got you interested in native plants?

Frank: Well, one of the reasons is, to collect some native plants, you have to go to places where other people don't go. I don't like to go where ten thousand other people have already been. I like to get off the trail.

Interviewer: So, you like the challenge of finding and collecting the plants?

Frank: Yep. And another thing is, if we don't collect native plants and try to preserve them, they won't exist. This would have other effects, too. Their pollinators would be affected, for example.

Interviewer: Pollinators?

Frank: Yeah, the specific type of insect, like a spider, a moth, or a fly of some kind that becomes the pollinator to a plant.

Interviewer: Meaning that the insect takes the pollen from one plant to another so the plants can reproduce.

Frank: That's right. And their pollinators have evolved along with the plants themselves, so the plants don't have to attract new pollinators in order to survive. But, if those pollinators die, then it's difficult for that plant to survive. That's why you'll see an article on some odd-looking fly or insect and you think, "Why do we need that?"

Interviewer: And there's a reason.

Frank: Yeah, there's a reason we need that fly, because it has a function. The opposite is true, too. If the species of plant dies, then its pollinator will no longer have a source of food and will also die, unless it can adapt very quickly.

Interviewer: Well, it must be so satisfying when you look around and see everything you've grown and cared for over the years.

Frank: It is. What's even more satisfying is to share them with other people who are also interested in native plants.

Interviewer: Vickie, how about you? What attracted you to gardening?

Vickie: Well, back in the '70s, when I was young, everyone was trying to be more green and natural and grow their own food. I just kind of had a knack for it.

Interviewer: What sort of plants were you growing?

Vickie: When I started, I only had a small apartment, so I was growing houseplants. And then I had an apartment with a patio, so I put tomato plants or some herbs out. And then, when I bought a house, I started to do more outside, and now what I do is mostly perennials. That's really my love now, the perennials.

Interviewer: Could you explain exactly what a perennial is?

Vickie: Well, perennials are plants that come back year after year. Annuals are the ones that die in the winter, and they don't come back. But with perennials, only the leaves and stems die in the winter. So in the spring – this is the really exciting part – the plants come back up again. Most perennials come back for years and years, and some, like irises, live longer than humans. You plant them and your grandchildren will have the same plants. That really appeals to me.

Interviewer: You know, you said that you have a knack for growing plants. Why is that? What makes your plants grow better?

Vickie: I guess it's what we call a "green thumb." But I think it's just an ability to notice little differences. You see a plant that's doing well in an environment, so you try to continue that kind of care. If you have a plant that's not doing well, you have to find out: Is there too much sun? Is there not enough sun? Is there enough water? Is there too much water?

Interviewer: People say gardening has a calming effect. Is that true?

Vickie: Well, it's true for me. I go out there and I get right down, put my hands into the dirt, pull the weeds, smell the plants, and I really can forget about my day-to-day troubles. When I'm in the garden, I don't think about the things that need to be done inside. And you're connected to the earth, which is why I like to have my hands right in there. And . . . it really ties me to that whole cycle of Earth's life. So for me, it's very calming.

Narrator: Now complete the steps in your book.

Narrator: Chapter 7, Life on Earth
Page 112
Listening for Examples, Step 1

Interviewer: Reggie, you went to the Galápagos Islands. How long did you stay?

Reggie: Well, I was there for five weeks doing conservation work. I decided to volunteer there because I'd heard so much about it . . . you know, we all dream about going to the Galápagos.

Interviewer: What is it about the Galápagos Islands that's so special?

Reggie: The number one reason why people really want to go to the Galápagos is the diversity of the wildlife. I mean, you don't have to go far before you see wildlife. For example, on the day I arrived, I was going from the airport and I saw Galápagos sea lions right away. I'd been there only 20 minutes and I saw sea lions. They were sleeping on benches meant for people!

Interviewer: I think of the Galápagos as having many unusual animals. Is that true?

Reggie: Well, there are animals in the Galápagos that don't exist anywhere else. This is because there are two ocean currents that come together at the Galápagos. One current comes from Antarctica, and it brings animals like penguins that come from colder climates. But the other current brings animals from warmer climates.

Interviewer: So part of the reason for the diversity is that these currents bring wildlife from different parts of the world.

Reggie: Right. So, I got to see a lot of animals. Many different kinds of birds, like blue-footed boobies, red-footed boobies, albatross . . . also pelicans, flamingos, the Galápagos penguins, like I said. The sea lions were everywhere. And I did a special trip to see different species of giant tortoise.

Interviewer: That sounds amazing!

Reggie: Yeah. But here's what surprised me. There's been a lot of environmental damage already, so the idea that it's an untouched environment is wrong. Let me give you an example: There used to be 13 subspecies of Galápagos giant tortoises, and now two are extinct. And a third is on the brink of extinction.

Interviewer: OK. Some people might ask, "Is there really a problem if a few species of tortoises disappear? We still have ten others." What would you say to those people?

Reggie: Well, I'd say that it shows a lack of understanding . . . because any ecosystem is so tightly bound together that even one small thing can change the balance and destroy the system. For instance, there's a tree that a particular bird relies on for food and shelter. If you destroy the tree, you lose the bird, and so on.

Interviewer: Do you think this has an effect on humans?

Reggie: Yes, of course. Um, there are places such as the Amazon jungle that are being cut and burned to make space for farmland. Right now, there are a lot of scientists doing research on plants that could have medicinal benefits. Maybe the cure for cancer is in a plant in the Amazon. But, if we cut down the trees . . .

Interviewer: We'll never find it.

Reggie: We'll never find it. Once it's gone, it's gone.

Narrator: Now complete the steps in your book.

Narrator: Chapter 7, Life on Earth
Page 117
Listening for Expressions of Contrast, Step 3

Narrator: One.

John Norris: Plants, for example, grow taller and wider throughout their lives. Animals start growing as soon as they are born but, unlike plants, usually stop growing when they become adults.

Narrator: Two.

John Norris: I'm sure you can think of many examples of different kinds of animal movement: walking, running, flying, swimming, crawling. Plants move, too, but not in the same way as animals.

Narrator: Three.

John Norris: Animals take in information about their environment by using their senses; in other words, they see, hear, smell, taste, and feel things around them. They use this information to react to their environment appropriately. Although plants do not have as many senses as animals, they do react to stimuli like water and light.

Narrator: Four.

John Norris: Plants have a very special way of getting food – they make it themselves. To make their own food, plants use a process called photosynthesis. During photosynthesis, plants combine carbon dioxide, water, and sunlight to make food. This food is stored inside the plant and used when the plant needs energy. Animals, on the other hand, cannot make their own food.

Narrator: Five.

John Norris: Respiration is a way of changing food into energy by using oxygen. Animals take in oxygen by breathing in air, whereas plants take in oxygen through tiny holes in their leaves.

Narrator: Six.

John Norris: During reproduction, plants and animals make more of their own kind. Animals have babies or lay eggs. In contrast, most plants make seeds, which fall into the soil and grow into a new plant.

Narrator: Now complete the steps in your book.

John Norris: You are probably familiar with the science of biology, which is the study of all living things in our biosphere. But what is a living thing? Scientists have a clear way of checking if something is living or nonliving. A scientist looks for seven life processes – seven special actions that all living things must do. The seven life processes are movement, reproduction, sensitivity, growth, nutrition, respiration, and excretion. These processes are like a checklist. If an organism has all seven, it's a living thing. If an organism is missing one or more of the processes, then it cannot be called a living thing. Now let's look at each life process in more detail.

I'll start with two life processes that are easy to observe and understand: growth and movement. All living things grow, which means that they increase in size. Plants, for example, grow taller and wider throughout their lives. Animals start growing as soon as they are born but, unlike plants, usually stop growing when they become adults. Living things also move. I'm sure you can think of many examples of different kinds of animal movement: walking, running, flying, swimming, crawling. Plants move, too, but not in the same way as animals. Plants move their roots down into the earth and their stems and leaves up toward the sky. Some flowers open in the morning and close at night. The movement of a plant is much slower than the movement of an animal, but both plants and animals move for the same reasons: to get food, to find a safe place to live, and to escape from dangerous situations.

The third life process is called sensitivity. What that means is that living things are sensitive to their environment. Animals take in information about their environment by using their senses; in other words, they see, hear, smell, taste, and feel things around them. They use this information to react to their environment appropriately. Although plants do not have as many senses as animals, they do react to stimuli like water and light. The sunflower got its name because it turns its face to follow the sun all day long. Some plants even respond to touch, such as the Venus flytrap.

Narrator: Now complete the steps in your book.

John Norris: The next two processes are nutrition and respiration. All living things need food, and the process of getting food is called nutrition. Plants have a very special way of getting food – they make it themselves. To make their own food, plants use a process called photosynthesis. During photosynthesis, plants combine carbon dioxide, water, and sunlight to make food. This food is stored inside the plant and used when the plant needs energy. Animals, on the other hand, cannot make their own food. Because of this, they have to eat plants, or eat other animals that have eaten plants.

Once food is inside a plant or animal, the next life process begins: respiration. Respiration is a way of changing food into energy by using oxygen. Animals take in oxygen by breathing in air, whereas plants take in oxygen through tiny holes in their leaves. Both plants and animals use the oxygen to change food into energy inside their bodies. All living things need energy to grow, to move, and to support all the other life processes, so you can see why nutrition and respiration are so important.

During respiration and in other life processes, plants and animals create waste materials. This waste needs to be removed or it can become harmful to the organism.

The process of removing waste materials is called excretion. Plants excrete, or remove, waste through small holes in their leaves and through their roots. Plants may also move the waste into a leaf, which then dies and falls off the plant. Animals move waste out of their bodies in their breath, sweat, urine, and feces.

To quickly summarize, then, all living things grow, move, react, eat, respire, and excrete. All living things also grow old and finally die, so the final life process – reproduction – is necessary if a species is to continue into the future. During reproduction, plants and animals make more of their own kind. Animals have babies or lay eggs. In contrast, most plants make seeds, which fall into the soil and grow into a new plant.

So in conclusion, for something to be called "living," it must show – or have the capability to show – evidence of all seven life processes: movement, growth, sensitivity, nutrition, respiration, excretion, and reproduction. Under most circumstances, we can easily identify something as living. But remember, it must perform all *seven* life processes. An automobile moves, an automobile can be sensitive, an automobile requires nutrition like gas, and it excretes carbon monoxide and smoke. But is it alive?

Narrator: Now complete the steps in your book.

8

**Narrator: Chapter 8, The Human Body
Page 123
Listening to Directions, Step 1**

Narrator: Task One.
Man: Put the palm of your right hand down on top of a desk or table, as shown in the picture. Keep your arm relaxed. Put your left hand on the upper part of your right arm. Now press gently down on the table with your right palm. Use your left hand to feel the muscles in your upper arm.

Now place your right palm under the desk or table. Push your hand gently up against the table. Use your left hand to feel the muscles in your upper arm.

Now answer the question in your book.

Narrator: Task Two.
Woman: Place your hands on your sides, just above your waist, so that you can feel your ribcage. Notice how your ribcage moves out when you breathe in, then falls back down when you breathe out. When you hear the beep, count the number of breaths you take in ten seconds. One "in" plus one "out" equals one breath. Try to breathe naturally, without changing or controlling your breathing rate. Are you ready? OK, start! [*beep*]

[*beep*] Stop. Write the number of breaths you took in your book. Multiply that number by 6. This is your average breathing rate per minute.

Narrator: Task Three.
Man: Find the pulse on the inside of your wrist. Place your first two fingers on your pulse point, as shown in the picture. Try to relax and let your fingers rest lightly on your pulse. When you hear the beep, count the number of beats you feel in 10 seconds. Are you ready? OK, start! [*beep*]

[*beep*] Stop. Write the number of beats you counted in your book. Multiply that number by 6. This is your average heartbeat.

Narrator: Task Four.
Woman: Do you know where your stomach is? Put your left hand over the spot where you think it is. Do not move your hand around. Are you ready? . . . Many people think the stomach is located in the center of the body, down by the navel. But in fact, it is higher up, on the left side of our body, closer to the chest. Your hand should be on the left side of your body, just below

where your ribcage ends. Did you find the right spot?

Narrator: This concludes the tasks.

Narrator: Chapter 8, The Human Body
   Page 127
   Listening for Main Ideas, Step 2

Interviewer: Becca, you were an athlete when you were a student, is that right?

Becca: Yes. I competed in track and field in college.

Interviewer: What kinds of training did you do?

Becca: The training? Well, the coaches really break it down into steps. So, the first step was a lot of weight lifting, like good, strong weight lifting. Then, the next step was cardiovascular training.

Interviewer: Which means building up your lungs and breathing better?

Becca: Breathing, yes, but also strengthening your heart and making your whole cardiovascular system work more efficiently. First, we would get a good base with three- to five-mile runs. After that, we did drills. With drills, you practice the running form, over and over and over again. This helps your body remember the best positions for running. Then, of course, there were the track workouts, as well.

Interviewer: And that's running around a track?

Becca: Yes. These are shorter distances, but faster and with breaks in between. To build our anaerobic power, the coach would have us run really hard for one minute, then take a break for five minutes, until we were fully rested, and then go right back into sprinting for another minute.

Interviewer: Can you explain what you mean by anaerobic power?

Becca: Anaerobic power. Well, *aerobic* means "oxygen," and the *an* means "without." So there are two energy systems in your body. One uses oxygen, and one does not. And the one that uses oxygen is mostly used in long-distance running, because you're running at a much slower pace, and your

body has the time to use the oxygen. But anaerobic energy is usually used for . . .

Interviewer: Short distances.

Becca: Right, like sprinting. There isn't time for the body to use oxygen, so it relies on the strength of your muscles.

Interviewer: So really, the muscles and the cardiovascular system are closely related.

Becca: Very closely, especially because, when you're running, your muscles need oxygen so that they can work. When you run, you start breathing faster and harder, right? That's because your muscles need more oxygen. So you breathe in more air, and the oxygen goes into your lungs and gets into your blood. Once in your blood, it travels to your muscles. The cardiovascular system and the muscular-skeletal system are very closely connected.

Interviewer: The skeletal system – do you actually try to strengthen your bones when you're training?

Becca: Yeah, the bones are just like muscles – they can get stronger with training. So when you look at top athletes, for example, their bones are significantly more dense than nonathletes' bones. Just like how your muscles get bigger when you lift more weight, your bones, by running, you put more stress on them, and they get stronger.

Narrator: Now complete the steps in your book.

Narrator: Chapter 8, The Human Body
   Page 129
   Listening for Specific Information, Step 3

Interviewer: Louise, you're a registered dietician. Why is good nutrition so important?

Louise: You need to eat to live, basically.

Interviewer: It's the basic idea, but people don't think about that.

Louise: Because I think more people, instead of eating to live, they live to eat, in a sense, because in our society, a lot of it is centered around food. You have a special event, and you go out for dinner. It's a holiday, so you buy some candy. A lot of our social events are centered around food, and I think that's part of the problem.

Interviewer: What's a healthier way to think about nutrition and food? How can people remember that we need to eat to live?

Louise: Just think of what your body really needs: your fiber, your vitamins and minerals, proteins, good fats, and carbohydrates. Those are your body's basic needs. So you should eat all of those things every day, but don't overindulge.

Interviewer: Do certain foods or kinds of food have specific benefits for different parts of the human body?

Louise: Yes, definitely. For example, the food that you eat can have a direct effect on your blood vessels. I talk to my patients about fiber, because fiber can help lower your cholesterol. If you have fiber in your diet and you also have some cholesterol in your diet, the fiber can actually pull the cholesterol away.

Interviewer: So that's good?

Louise: Yes, it's good because cholesterol is what clogs our blood vessels.

Interviewer: Now, how about protein?

Louise: Well, proteins have a lot of different functions, but mostly you need proteins for your body to grow, and to build body tissue and muscles. That's the main role, to build and repair our muscles.

Interviewer: And carbohydrates and fats?

Louise: Those are your energy sources. We need a lot of energy every day, so that's why carbs are so important. And I know people think fats are bad, but you need fats to help protect your organs and to provide energy, too.

Interviewer: Are there foods you can eat to build strong bones?

Louise: For bones, you should look at calcium and vitamin D. Those go hand-in-hand. You always hear about calcium because that's basically what makes your bones. But you need vitamin D to absorb the calcium and to transport it throughout your body. You also need protein to build strong bones.

Interviewer: You know, it sounds like you can't eat only one kind of food. You need to have the mix.

Louise: Yes, exactly. And to be healthy, you have to have good eating habits, but also exercise. I cannot stress that enough.

Interviewer: Louise, I feel like there's so much need for this type of knowledge right now. I'm just thinking of all of the nutritional problems that Americans are having.

Louise: Mm-hm. I really enjoy helping people with the little things that can help them in their everyday life: Eat breakfast. Drink water. Cut back on coffee. Small, easy steps that people can see making a difference. That's empowering.

Narrator: Now complete the steps in your book.

Narrator: Chapter 8, The Human Body
Page 133
Note Taking: Listening for Expressions of Time Order, Step 2

Narrator: One.

Larry Fontanilla: This phase can last for several hours, and when it's over, the food has become a thick soup.

Narrator: Two.

Larry Fontanilla: From the stomach, the food then moves into the small intestine, where something very important happens.

Narrator: Three.

Larry Fontanilla: Finally, the remaining dry waste, or feces, moves out of the large intestine and out of the body.

Narrator: Four.

Larry Fontanilla: When we breathe, air enters our body through our mouth and nose. Next, it travels through an airway called the trachea into the lungs.

Narrator: Five.

Larry Fontanilla: After entering our blood, oxygen is transported to every part of the body, where our cells use it to carry out life functions.

Narrator: Six.

Larry Fontanilla: Finally, the oxygenated blood returns to the heart, ready to begin the cycle again.

Narrator: Now complete the steps in your book.

Narrator: Chapter 8, The Human Body
Page 135
Note Taking: Taking Notes in a Flow Chart, Step 2

Larry Fontanilla: Have you ever thought about all the things that happen inside your body? The human body, like all living organisms, is made up of cells. Cells form tissues, and tissues form organs. Finally, several organs that work together form a body system, which is the topic of our lecture today. You know, humans have 11 different body systems! Together, these systems carry out every function that your body needs. When your body is healthy, its systems work together smoothly and efficiently. But if even one of the 11 systems breaks down, you cannot survive.

Today, I'd like to focus on the digestive system, the cardiovascular system, and the respiratory system. These three systems deliver life-giving oxygen and nutrients to every part of the body. Each system works independently to perform its own unique functions, but they also interact with each other in important ways.

Now, we all like to eat, so let's start with the digestive system. Our bodies use the energy in the food we eat to carry out all of our life functions. The process of breaking down food and releasing its nutrients into the body is called digestion.

Digestion begins when you put food into your mouth. As your mouth moves and chews the food, it becomes softer and breaks apart into smaller pieces. When the pieces of food are small and soft enough to swallow, they travel down a pipe, called the esophagus, from your mouth to your stomach. The stomach's powerful muscles squeeze and mix the food with chemicals.

This phase can last for several hours, and when it's over, the food has become a thick soup. From the stomach, the food then moves into the small intestine, where something very important happens. Nutrients pass from the food through the intestine and into the blood. Those nutrients have now become part of the cardiovascular system, which I'll talk about in a minute.

After the small intestine takes out all the nutrients, the leftover food moves into the large intestine. Here, the intestine absorbs most of the water from the food. Finally, the remaining dry waste, or feces, moves out of the large intestine and out of the body. The whole process of digestion, from mouth to large intestine, takes about 24 hours to complete.

Narrator: Now complete the steps in your book.

Narrator: Chapter 8, The Human Body
Page 137
Note Taking: Taking Notes in a Flow Chart, Step 3

Larry Fontanilla: Now, the job of the respiratory system is to bring oxygen from the air into the body. Like food, oxygen is necessary for life. When we breathe, air enters our body through our mouth and nose. Next, it travels through an airway called the trachea into the lungs. The air that enters our lungs is rich with oxygen. Inside the lungs, an important gas exchange takes place: Oxygen in the air passes into our blood, and at the same time, carbon dioxide from our blood passes into our lungs. That carbon dioxide travels back out of our lungs and through the trachea, to be exhaled, or breathed out through the mouth and nose.

After entering our blood, oxygen is transported to every part of the body, where our cells use it to carry out life functions. We need to breathe about eight liters of air every minute to stay alive, and even more when we exercise. Without oxygen, we would die in just a few minutes.

By now, you've probably figured out that blood has many important roles. It transports nutrients from food and oxygen to the rest of our body. Blood makes up one part of our cardiovascular system, along with the heart and our blood vessels. There are two main kinds of blood vessels in our bodies: arteries and veins. Arteries carry blood from the heart to the body, and veins carry blood from the body back to the heart. The heart is the source of power in the cardiovascular system. With every beat, the heart pushes blood on its cycle around the body.

When blood first leaves the heart, it's carrying a lot of oxygen. Arteries carry this oxygenated blood all over the body. One of the places the blood goes to is our small intestine, where it picks up nutrients from food. As blood travels around the body, it gives oxygen and nutrients to each cell. At the same time, it picks up waste from the cells. When the oxygen in our blood has been used up, the veins carry it back to the heart. When blood enters the heart, it is immediately pumped into the lungs to get fresh oxygen from the respiratory system. Finally, the oxygenated blood returns to the heart, ready to begin the cycle again. The entire cycle – from heart to body and back to heart, to lungs and back to heart – takes only 20 seconds.

These three systems – digestive, respiratory, and cardiovascular – work together to maintain life. The digestive system brings nutrients into the body. The respiratory system brings oxygen into the body. The cardiovascular system carries nutrients and oxygen to the cells. Today, we talked about only three of the body's 11 systems. When you consider that there are eight more equally important systems, you can see that the human body is truly an extraordinary organism.

Narrator: Now complete the steps in your book.

9

Narrator: Chapter 9, Living Longer, Living Better?
Page 141
Recording and Calculating Numbers, Step 2

Narrator: Start with the number 75 – this is your "starting age." Then add or subtract the correct number of years for each of the following questions . . . . One.
Woman: If you are female, add 4. If you are male, subtract 3. Write your new total in the first blank, under *Calculator*.

Narrator: Two.
Woman: If any of your grandparents lived to the age of 85 or older, add 2. If your grandparents are younger than 85, do not make any changes to your total.

Narrator: Three.
Woman: If anyone in your family has had cancer, subtract 1.

Narrator: Four.
Woman: If anyone in your family has had a heart problem, subtract 1.

Narrator: Five.
Woman: If you live in a big city, subtract 2. If you live in a small town, add 1.

Narrator: Six.
Woman: If you exercise for 20 to 30 minutes at least 3 times per week, add 3.

Narrator: Seven.
Woman: If you usually sleep 6 to 8 hours, add 2. If you usually get fewer than 6 hours of sleep, subtract 3.

Narrator: Eight.
Woman: If you are basically satisfied with your life, add 2. If you are often unhappy about your life, subtract 2.

Narrator: Nine.
Woman: If you get angry easily, subtract 3. If you do not get angry easily, add 2.

Narrator: Ten.

Woman: If you do not have any close friends, subtract 2.

Narrator: Now complete the steps in your book.

Narrator: Chapter 9, Living Longer, Living Better?
Page 143
Listening for Details, Step 3

Interviewer: Anna, you've been a registered nurse for 11 years. You work in a geriatrics clinic.

Anna: Yes. I provide care to patients who are 65 and older.

Interviewer: In your work, have you noticed that people are living longer?

Anna: Definitely, yes. Just ten years ago, most of our patients were in their 70s and 80s, and now most are in their 90s. And every now and then, we have a patient who's 100 or 101. When I started this job, I'd never seen anyone that old!

Interviewer: And you've seen that change in just ten years. Do you know what's causing this increase in longevity?

Anna: Partly, it's better nutrition. Even though we eat a lot of fast food, it's much easier for people to get their basic nutritional needs than it was 100 years ago. Also, medical advances, like immunizations . . . just the improved medical care that we have. And education plays a part.

Interviewer: Education?

Anna: I think people today are more aware that they need to take care of themselves and prepare for growing old.

Interviewer: But there are still some disadvantages of getting older, aren't there?

Anna: Absolutely. I see a lot of elderly people who lose their independence, and that can be devastating. They lose their ability to walk, or maybe they can't see as well, so they need someone to take care of them all the time. And older people have a higher risk for certain diseases that are more common with aging, like diabetes and Alzheimer's.

Interviewer: Do you think that someday doctors will be able to control the human life span?

Anna: Oh, yes. I have no doubt that doctors will figure it out.

Interviewer: And do you think that it's a good thing to extend the human life span?

Anna: Maybe. It depends. I think it would only be a good thing if doctors can make sure that the quality of an extended life span is good. But if living longer means expanding the period of time when you can't even do the basic activities of daily living, like brushing your teeth, getting dressed, or taking a bath on your own, then that is . . .

Interviewer: Not a benefit.

Anna: . . . not a benefit. It wouldn't help people at all.

Interviewer: You know, I think most people just assume that of course, living longer is always a good thing. But it's more complicated than that, isn't it?

Anna: I used to think, "Oh, I want to live to be 100." But now, after working in geriatrics for 11 years, I'm not so sure. Part of me doesn't want to live to be 100. Not unless I can make the years between 90 and 100 quality years. I'm taking good care of myself now so that I have a better chance of that happening.

Narrator: Now complete the steps in your book.

Narrator: Chapter 9, Living Longer, Living Better?
Page 145
Listening for Specific Information, Step 2

Interviewer: Hi, Jericho. You're still in high school, right?

Jericho: Yes. I'm eighteen years old.

Interviewer: Well, maybe you haven't thought too much about this topic yet, but you might have heard that in the United States, average life expectancy for a man is 74 years. What do you think about that?

Jericho: I didn't know that. That actually sounds a little young to me. Maybe around, like, 85 to 90 – I feel like that's closer. Seventy-four is kind of young.

Interviewer: It's interesting that you say that because 74 is the life expectancy now, but there are a lot of predictions that people of your generation will live longer than that.

Jericho: Well, there'll probably be new technology and new ways to eat that'll make life healthier and a lot longer.

Interviewer: Not only that, but researchers are looking for a gene in humans that affects our aging. And by changing this gene, they hope to extend the human life span – maybe to as much as 120 years. Do you think that's a good idea?

Jericho: You know, honestly, I think there are some advantages and disadvantages to that. Advantages are, you get to see your children and your grandchildren grow up. You'll see society change. But disadvantages are, when it does happen, I think it's going to be really expensive. So living longer will only be for people who can pay. And the people who can't afford it, they'll pass on earlier. That's not fair.

Interviewer: So you wouldn't want to extend your life span?

Jericho: I think it delays the inevitable. We're all going to have to pass on someday. I just want to live my life – live it to the best, just have fun, do everything right – and when I need to pass on, I'll pass on. I don't want to have my life extended.

Interviewer: Well, if you do live naturally to 120 years old, you'll still be here in 100 years. Can you imagine some of the things you might see then? Will society be a better place in 100 years, do you think?

Jericho: Yes, I think so. I think technology will be really advanced. We'll have a lot of new high-tech products to make life convenient. We might even have the technology to live on the moon. Maybe we'll have a more stable and more perfect government in our nation. Maybe we'll find different ways to produce food rather than taking it from the earth and killing animals, stuff like that.

Interviewer: So you sound pretty positive about the future.

Jericho: Yeah. My parents always tell me, there are so many things that I have now that they never had – you know, technology, medicine, computers, Internet . . . discoveries like cures for certain types of cancer. And if my life is easier now, just think how much easier my children's lives will be.

Narrator: Now complete the steps in your book.

Narrator: **Chapter 9, Living Longer, Living Better? Page 146 Listening for Specific Information, Step 2**

Interviewer: Eleanor, you turned 81 years old this month, is that right?

Eleanor: Yes, I just had my birthday.

Interviewer: You are such an energetic, positive person, Eleanor, that I wanted to ask you if you have a secret for staying so active in your 80s.

Eleanor: Well, doctors have found that people who remain mentally alert and physically active do often live longer. So I keep active in many ways. I'm a member of several organizations and clubs. I like to go out at least once a day to do something and talk to other people. I enjoy learning, so sometimes I'll take a class at the university. And I love to read – I read two newspapers a day, and several magazines.

Interviewer: You really *do* keep busy!

Eleanor: And lots of friends, of course. And most of all, I have a wonderful family. Family relationships are very important because they offer so much support. A lot of older people without families, I think they feel more stress. They may feel lonely and left out. I have 5 children and 13 grandchildren. So naturally, I spend a lot of time with them.

Interviewer: When you think about your grandchildren, do you feel optimistic? Do you think that the world is going to be a better place for them?

Eleanor: I think their biggest challenge will be the problems caused by overpopulation. I've seen the world population go from 2 billion to 4 billion to 6 billion in my lifetime. It's the number one problem facing the entire world. Already we can't provide enough food and housing for the billions that we have.

Interviewer: And the population keeps increasing.

Eleanor: Oh, yes. They're expecting more than 10 billion by 2050!

Interviewer: So it sounds like the future may not be a very good place.

Eleanor: Well, on the other hand, the human mind is so amazing. In just the last 100 years or so, we've made the telephone, the car, the television, the computer. I've seen all these things come to pass. And what is going to happen in the next 100 years? We have no way of knowing.

Interviewer: I'd like to think that the future will be better in some ways.

Eleanor: Oh, me, too! My father was always looking to the future and wanted to make the world better for young people. I think I got that attitude from him. I try to look forward. I would love to be here 100 years from now. What is our world going to be like? What can I do to help it?

Interviewer: So if you could live for 100 more years, would you?

Eleanor: Of course! There are so many interesting things coming up. I want to see who's going to be riding in the spaceships!

Narrator: Now complete the steps in your book.

Narrator: Chapter 9, Living Longer, Living Better? Page 150 Listening for Speculative Language, Step 2

Narrator: One.

Mahealani Kaneshiro-Pineiro: Of course, the environment that you grow up in and your lifestyle also influence things like your body shape and your personality.

Narrator: Two.

Mahealani Kaneshiro-Pineiro: Scientists also think that genes may play a role in determining how long we can live.

Narrator: Three.

Mahealani Kaneshiro-Pineiro: In 2003, a group of international scientists called the Human Genome Organization succeeded in analyzing human DNA for the first time.

Narrator: Four.

Mahealani Kaneshiro-Pineiro: For example, the scientists learned which specific genes carry diseases like breast cancer, diabetes, Alzheimer's disease, and cystic fibrosis. By studying the human genome more, they might soon find ways to treat and even prevent these diseases.

Narrator: Five.

Mahealani Kaneshiro-Pineiro: But many researchers believe that gene therapy will soon become a common way of preventing and curing disease.

Narrator: Six.

Mahealani Kaneshiro-Pineiro: Studies of certain insects, worms, and mice have found genes that seem to allow these organisms to live longer.

Narrator: Now complete the steps in your book.

Narrator: Chapter 9, Living Longer, Living Better? Page 151 Note Taking: Evaluating Your Own Note Taking, Step 2

Mahealani Kaneshiro-Pineiro: DNA is a molecule that's found inside most cells in the human body. DNA carries the genetic information that determines what you will look like and also other qualities that you will have. But, let me begin by describing where DNA is in your body.

You already know that the human body is made up of trillions of cells. Inside most of those cells is a small, round structure called the nucleus. The nucleus is sometimes also called the "control center" of the cell. If you go inside the nucleus of a human body cell, you will find many chromosomes – 46 of them, to be exact. Most chromosomes look like Xs, but in fact, they are made of long, thin strands that form X shapes. These long, thin strands are your DNA.

A DNA molecule is shaped like a ladder that has been twisted. This is where you can find your genes, in the "steps" of the DNA ladder. Genes are small sections of your DNA that give instructions to your cells. Your genes have two very important jobs. First, they tell every cell in your body what its job is going to be. For example, is the cell going to become a muscle cell? A brain cell? Will it be part of an organ? Part of a bone? Each cell follows the instructions in your genes to build the human body, and to carry out all of the body's functions.

The second important job that genes do, and the one you may be more familiar with, is decide what you will look like. In other words, genes decide your personal traits, such as your eye, hair, and skin color, the shape and size of your body and your face, and even your personality. Of course, the environment that you grow up in and your lifestyle also influence things like your body shape and your personality, but your genes determine your basic characteristics before you are even born.

So where do your genes come from? They come from your parents. I said before that every cell has 46 chromosomes. Half of them come from your mother, and half come from your father. That is why you look and act similarly to your parents. But each set of chromosomes combines differently in each person, which is why you are not an exact copy of your parents.

Narrator: Now complete the steps in your book.

Mahealani Kaneshiro-Pineiro: Now, what do genes and DNA have to do with the human life span, our main topic today? A lot, actually. Genes carry information about what kinds of diseases we are likely to get. Scientists also think that genes may play a role in determining how long we can live. Because of this, DNA research may be the next big step in extending and improving the human life span.

In 2003, a group of international scientists called the Human Genome Organization succeeded in analyzing human DNA for the first time. They studied almost all of the genes found in our DNA, about 25,000 different genes. Although the group still doesn't know exactly what each of those genes does, they have learned a lot of information that can help humans live longer and stay healthier. For example, the scientists learned which specific genes carry diseases like breast cancer, diabetes, Alzheimer's disease, and cystic fibrosis. By studying the human genome more, they might soon find ways to treat and even prevent these diseases.

Information from the Human Genome Project will also help scientists improve gene therapy. What is gene therapy, exactly? Well, for example, imagine that you had a gene that increased your chances of getting cancer. Now, imagine if doctors were able to remove that gene and replace it with a new gene that does not carry cancer. Doctors can't cure cancer with gene therapy yet – and it's still a controversial area of medicine – but many researchers believe that gene therapy will soon become a common way of preventing and curing disease.

Finally, what can the human genome tell us about getting old? Is there an "aging gene" – a gene in our DNA that determines how long we will live? Probably. Scientists know that nongenetic factors – our environment, nutrition, exercise, sleep, stress, and other aspects of our lifestyle – affect our health and our life span. At the same time, scientists also know that people who live for a very long time tend to have children who live for a very long time. That is, it looks like longevity can be inherited. Furthermore, studies of certain insects, worms, and mice have found genes that seem to allow these organisms to live longer. The genetics of human aging is certainly an exciting topic in science today, so it can't be much longer before more information is discovered.

Narrator: Now complete the steps in your book.

Lecture Quizzes
and Quiz Answers

Name _____   Date _____

Chapter **1** LECTURE QUIZ

PART 1 True/False Questions (50 points)

Decide if the following statements are true (T) or false (F).

_____ **1** Earth is made up of four main layers.

_____ **2** Earth is more than 4 billion years old.

_____ **3** Earth is the densest planet in the solar system.

_____ **4** In general, Earth's temperature increases as you go down from the surface toward the center of the planet.

_____ **5** The main topic of this lecture is Earth's place in the solar system.

PART 2 Multiple Choice Questions (50 points)

Circle the best answer from the choices listed.

1 The thickest layer of Earth's structure is the _____.
 a oceanic crust
 b continental crust
 c mantle
 d core

2 Earth is the only planet that has _____ on its surface.
 a liquid water
 b liquid rock
 c mountains
 d crust

3 Scientists use _____ to learn about Earth's internal structure.
 a ocean waves
 b seismic waves
 c liquid rock
 d fruit

4 Most of Earth's surface is covered by _____.
 a forests
 b layers
 c continental crust
 d oceanic crust

5 The movement of Earth's crust causes all of the following *except* _____.
 a earthquakes
 b mountains
 c oceans
 d valleys

6 The upper part of the mantle is _____.
 a hot and soft
 b cool and solid
 c made of iron and nickel
 d under high pressure

7 The mantle is about _____ kilometers thick.
 a 6–11
 b 30–40
 c 2,900
 d 13,000

8 A unique feature of _____ is that it has liquid rock.
 a the outer core
 b the inner core
 c the crust
 d Mars

9 _____ is an inner planet.
 a Earth
 b Mercury
 c Venus
 d all of the above

10 The hottest part of Earth is the _____.
 a crust
 b upper mantle
 c lower mantle
 d inner core

Chapter **2** LECTURE QUIZ

PART 1 True/False Questions (50 points)

Decide if the following statements are true (T) or false (F).

_____ **1** There are about 75 volcanoes on the surface of Earth.

_____ **2** Volcanoes usually erupt suddenly, without giving any warning signs.

_____ **3** Supervolcanoes are the rarest and most dangerous type of volcano.

_____ **4** Dr. Fryer doesn't like volcanoes because they are scary.

_____ **5** Dr. Fryer talks about four basic types of volcanoes in her lecture.

PART 2 Multiple Choice Questions (50 points)

Circle the best answer from the choices listed.

1 According to Dr. Fryer, there are about _____ volcanic eruptions every day.
  a 20
  b 75
  c 80
  d 150

2 Liquid rock on the surface of Earth is called _____.
  a magma
  b ash
  c vent
  d lava

3 Volcanic eruptions are usually started by _____.
  a pressure
  b gases
  c high temperatures
  d earthquakes

4 A narrow passageway through Earth's mantle is called _____.
  a magma
  b the throat
  c a vent
  d an eruption

5 An example of a shield volcano is _____.
  a Toba
  b the Big Island
  c Mauna Loa
  d Mt. Fuji

6 Composite volcanoes have _____.
  a a sloping shape
  b bowl-shaped craters
  c alternating layers
  d the most explosive eruptions

7 Cinders are _____.
  a small pieces of hardened lava
  b small, bowl-shaped volcanoes
  c groups of volcanoes close together
  d fast-growing volcanoes

8 When the Toba volcano erupted, _____.
  a 75,000 people died
  b more than half of the people on Earth died
  c all life on Earth died
  d a big, cone-shaped volcano was formed

9 The least dangerous type of volcano is probably the _____ volcano.
  a shield
  b composite
  c cinder cone
  d super

10 Dr. Fryer mentions all of the following warning signs *except* _____.
  a cracks in the ground
  b loud noises
  c melting glaciers
  d the taste of drinking water

Chapter 3 LECTURE QUIZ

PART 1 True/False Questions (50 points)

Decide if the following statements are true (T) or false (F).

_____ 1 Most of the water covering Earth's surface is drinking water.

_____ 2 According to the lecture, farms are located near rivers so that the animals can drink the water.

_____ 3 The most serious problem affecting Earth's water supply is water pollution.

_____ 4 In 20 years, there will be fewer people using water on Earth than there are now.

_____ 5 The lecturer believes all people must work together to protect Earth's water supply.

PART 2 Multiple Choice Questions (50 points)

Circle the best answer from the choices listed.

1 The main topic of this lecture is _____ water.
   a salt
   b ice
   c surface
   d ground

2 _____ of water on Earth is freshwater in liquid form.
   a Less than 1 percent
   b About 3 percent
   c About 25 percent
   d About 75 percent

3 When water first starts to flow permanently on Earth's surface, it is called _____.
   a rain
   b a stream
   c a river
   d a lake

4 Water usually stays on Earth's surface when _____.
   a there is a canyon cut into the land
   b it is snowing
   c two streams combine into a river
   d the ground is already full of water

5 Water carries a lot of _____, which can help make land more _____.
   a salt, fertile
   b pollution, rich
   c nutrients, dry
   d nutrients, fertile

6 Washing dishes, washing clothes, and bathing are all examples of _____.
   a irrigation
   b transportation
   c farming activities
   d daily tasks

7 The process of bringing freshwater to dry areas for farming is called _____.
   a irrigation
   b transportation
   c industrialization
   d fertilization

8 The lecturer discusses all of the following threats to water *except* _____.
   a loss of natural environment
   b pollution
   c global warming
   d overuse by humans

9 Air pollution that falls to Earth in drops of water is called _____.
   a pesticide
   b acid rain
   c critical water
   d fertilizer

10 The problems discussed in the lecture are caused by _____.
   a animals
   b humans
   c nature
   d all of the above

Chapter 4 LECTURE QUIZ

PART 1 True/False Questions (50 points)

Decide if the following statements are true (T) or false (F).

_____ 1 Most of Earth's oceans are located in the southern half of the planet.

_____ 2 The biggest and deepest ocean is located between Europe and North America.

_____ 3 The largest layer of the ocean is the middle layer.

_____ 4 As you go down into the ocean, pressure increases, but temperature and light decrease.

_____ 5 The lecturer probably believes that scientists will learn a lot of new information about the ocean in the future.

PART 2 Multiple Choice Questions (50 points)

Circle the best answer from the choices listed.

1 The northernmost ocean is the _____ ocean.
  a Pacific
  b Atlantic
  c Indian
  d Arctic

2 All oceans and seas on Earth are _____.
  a deep
  b connected
  c dense
  d pitch black

3 Which of the following is NOT true of the surface layer?
  a Its nickname is the "sunlit zone."
  b Many algae and plants live there.
  c It is very dense.
  d Its average temperature is 15°C.

4 Animals swim from the middle layer to the surface layer _____.
  a to find food
  b because they like warm temperatures
  c for exercise
  d to use special adaptations

5 The midnight zone begins around _____ meters deep.
  a 100
  b 200
  c 1,000
  d 3,800

6 Water temperature changes most quickly in the _____.
  a surface layer
  b middle layer
  c bottom layer
  d middle and bottom layers

7 A fish gives off its own light. This is an example of _____.
  a marine life
  b algae
  c an ocean layer
  d a special adaptation

8 Pressure is greatest _____.
  a above the ocean
  b at the ocean's surface
  c in the middle layer
  d at the bottom of the ocean

9 One atmosphere is equal to _____ kilogram(s) per square centimeter.
  a 1
  b 10
  c 600
  d 1,000

10 The lecturer talks about all of the following topics except _____.
  a threats to Earth's oceans
  b water pressure
  c ocean structure
  d marine life

Chapter **5** LECTURE QUIZ

PART 1 True/False Questions (50 points)

Decide if the following statements are true (T) or false (F).

_____ **1** According to this lecture, the air is empty.

_____ **2** Nitrogen and oxygen together make up 99 percent of the air.

_____ **3** A humidity level of 10 percent means there is not much water in the air.

_____ **4** Air with any amount of particulate matter is polluted.

_____ **5** Particulate matter in the air can cause health problems and other negative effects.

PART 2 Multiple Choice Questions (50 points)

Circle the best answer from the choices listed.

1 There are _____ gases in the air.
 a 10
 b 12
 c 21
 d 78

2 Gases that make up the air sometimes have a strong _____.
 a color
 b smell
 c taste
 d none of the above

3 Water in gas form is called _____.
 a vapor
 b liquid
 c arid
 d oxygen

4 When air contains 25 percent of the total possible amount of water it can hold, then the humidity level is _____.
 a 25 percent
 b 50 percent
 c 75 percent
 d 100 percent

5 All of the following are mentioned as sources of water in the air *except* _____.
 a humans
 b clouds
 c plants
 d the ground

6 Particulate matter is tiny pieces of _____ that are floating in the air.
 a gas
 b liquid matter
 c solid matter
 d vapor

7 The lecturer discusses two kinds of particulate matter, natural and _____.
 a active
 b man-made
 c volcanic
 d pollution

8 If your nose starts itching when you smell some flowers, it is probably caused by _____.
 a salt
 b dirt
 c pollen
 d viruses

9 An example of human activity that creates particulate matter is _____.
 a swimming
 b sneezing
 c walking
 d driving a car

10 The lecturer's main message is: People should _____.
 a move to humid areas
 b avoid particulate matter
 c not burn fossil fuels
 d think about what is in the air

Chapter 6 LECTURE QUIZ

PART 1 True/False Questions (50 points)

Decide if the following statements are true (T) or false (F).

_____ **1** Greenhouse gases have always been a part of Earth's atmosphere.

_____ **2** Earth's average surface temperature has doubled in the past 150 years.

_____ **3** The greenhouse effect is always bad for Earth.

_____ **4** The lecturer believes that global warming is caused by an increase in the greenhouse effect.

_____ **5** The lecturer believes it is too late to stop global warming.

PART 2 Multiple Choice Questions (50 points)

Circle the best answer from the choices listed.

1 Greenhouse gases cause the atmosphere to _____.
  a mix
  b move
  c expand
  d warm up

2 The radiation that enters the top of Earth's atmosphere comes from _____.
  a carbon dioxide
  b the ozone layer
  c the sun
  d Earth's surface

3 Greenhouse gases stop heat energy from _____.
  a entering the ocean
  b returning to space
  c being absorbed by Earth
  d staying in the atmosphere

4 The natural greenhouse effect makes Earth's climate _____.
  a hot
  b polluted
  c pleasant
  d dry

5 In the past 100 years, the greenhouse effect has become stronger because of _____.
  a human activity
  b rising sea level
  c global warming
  d radiation

6 _____ is *not* mentioned as a possible cause of the rising sea level.
  a Ocean expansion
  b Severe weather
  c Melting snow
  d The Greenland ice cap

7 In the past 40 years, _____ have doubled.
  a areas experiencing drought
  b changes in the weather
  c stronger hurricanes
  d melting glaciers

8 Not all scientists agree that _____.
  a greenhouse gases are increasing
  b the Greenland ice cap is melting
  c the ocean level is rising
  d Earth's surface is getting warmer

9 According to the lecture, the sea level may rise another _____ centimeters in the twenty-first century.
  a 15–25
  b 45
  c 60
  d 90

10 The lecturer feels that global warming is a(n) _____ issue.
  a ethical
  b educational
  c financial
  d all of the above

Chapter **7** LECTURE QUIZ

PART 1 True/False Questions (50 points)

Decide if the following statements are true (T) or false (F).

_____ **1** Scientists are not sure how to check if something is living or nonliving.

_____ **2** Both plants and animals have the same reasons for moving.

_____ **3** Plants can react to stimuli such as water, light, and touch.

_____ **4** Plants directly or indirectly provide food for all animals on Earth.

_____ **5** According to the lecturer, a car is a living thing because it performs all seven life processes.

PART 2 Multiple Choice Questions (50 points)

Circle the best answer from the choices listed.

1 If something is missing one of the seven life processes, it is considered to be _____.
 a nonliving
 b living
 c an organism
 d special

2 Plant movement is _____ than animal movement.
 a wider
 b taller
 c slower
 d stranger

3 An example of plant movement is _____.
 a walking
 b flying
 c crawling
 d opening

4 All of the following are reasons for animal movement *except* _____.
 a getting food
 b making food
 c finding shelter
 d running away from danger

5 Animals use their _____ to gather information about their environment.
 a senses
 b stimuli
 c reaction
 d growth

6 The lecturer talks about the sunflower as an example of the process of _____.
 a movement
 b sensitivity
 c nutrition
 d growth

7 Because all organisms need energy, _____ are especially important processes.
 a growth and movement
 b nutrition and respiration
 c respiration and reproduction
 d nutrition and excretion

8 Combining carbon dioxide, water, and sunlight to make food is called _____.
 a respiration
 b reaction
 c photosynthesis
 d conversion

9 Animals get oxygen _____.
 a by eating plants
 b through tiny holes
 c by changing food into energy
 d by breathing

10 The purpose of reproduction is to _____.
 a get rid of waste materials
 b enjoy time with children
 c make different kinds of organisms
 d continue the species

Chapter 8 LECTURE QUIZ

PART 1 True/False Questions (50 points)

Decide if the following statements are true (T) or false (F).

_____ 1 The building blocks of the human body, from simplest to most complex, are: cells, tissues, organs, and systems.

_____ 2 Each human body system works independently to carry out all of the life processes.

_____ 3 The main job of the respiratory system is to move blood through the body.

_____ 4 The blood in arteries is oxygenated, but the blood in veins is not.

_____ 5 The lecturer feels that the digestive, respiratory, and cardiovascular systems are the three most important systems in the human body.

PART 2 Multiple Choice Questions (50 points)

Circle the best answer from the choices listed.

1 There are _____ human body systems.
 a one
 b three
 c seven
 d eleven

2 Food is important for the body because it _____.
 a contains oxygen
 b contains nutrients
 c tastes delicious
 d is always healthy

3 The correct order in digestion is _____.
 a mouth, esophagus, stomach
 b mouth, trachea, stomach
 c stomach, large intestine, small intestine
 d none of the above

4 Food becomes a thick soup in the _____.
 a mouth
 b small intestine
 c stomach
 d feces

5 Nutrients become part of the cardiovascular system in the _____.
 a esophagus
 b stomach
 c small intestine
 d large intestine

6 The mouth is part of the _____ system.
 a digestive
 b respiratory
 c both a and b
 d neither a nor b

7 One important function of breathing is to _____.
 a carry blood to the lungs
 b bring water to the stomach
 c pump blood to the heart
 d exhale carbon dioxide from the body

8 The cardiovascular system is made up of the heart, blood, and _____.
 a blood vessels
 b arteries
 c veins
 d oxygen

9 Blood goes to the small intestine in order to get _____.
 a waste
 b nutrients
 c fresh oxygen
 d cells

10 It takes _____ for blood to travel around the entire body.
 a about 20 seconds
 b a few minutes
 c 8 minutes
 d about 20 minutes

Chapter 9 LECTURE QUIZ

PART 1 True/False Questions (50 points)

Decide if the following statements are true (T) or false (F).

_____ 1 DNA, as well as your environment and lifestyle choices, influences your physical appearance and personality.

_____ 2 One function of genes is to determine the role of each cell in the human body.

_____ 3 When the Human Genome Organization (HGO) analyzed human DNA, it found about 25,000 different genes.

_____ 4 The HGO used information from human DNA to cure cancer and other diseases.

_____ 5 The lecturer is against gene therapy because she thinks it is too dangerous.

PART 2 Multiple Choice Questions (50 points)

Circle the best answer from the choices listed.

1 A human body cell has _____ chromosomes.
   a 23
   b 46
   c 25,000
   d trillions of

2 A cell's control center is called the _____.
   a chromosome
   b strand
   c nucleus
   d molecule

3 The shape of a DNA molecule is _____.
   a small and round
   b long and fat
   c similar to a ladder
   d influenced by the environment

4 People get their genes from _____.
   a the environment
   b scientists
   c the nucleus
   d their parents

5 Right now, doctors can learn _____ from our genes.
   a which diseases we are likely to get
   b how long we will live
   c how long our children will live
   d none of the above

6 During gene therapy, genes that increase a person's risk of disease are replaced with _____.
   a mouse DNA
   b new genes
   c his or her parents' genes
   d the aging gene

7 All of the following are examples of non-genetic factors except _____.
   a exercise habits
   b stress level
   c sleep patterns
   d eye color

8 Very old people usually have _____.
   a many health problems
   b strong DNA
   c children who also live for a long time
   d good nutrition

9 Scientists have found genes that affect aging in _____.
   a insects
   b children
   c old people
   d all humans

10 The lecturer feels _____ about the future of genetic research.
   a excited
   b worried
   c confused
   d negative

Lecture Quiz Answers

Chapter 1

PART 1

1 F
2 T
3 T
4 T
5 F

PART 2

1 d
2 a
3 b
4 d
5 c

6 b
7 c
8 a
9 d
10 d

Chapter 2

PART 1

1 F
2 F
3 T
4 F
5 T

PART 2

1 a
2 d
3 d
4 b
5 c

6 c
7 a
8 b
9 a
10 b

Chapter 3

PART 1

1 F
2 F
3 F
4 F
5 T

PART 2

1 c
2 a
3 b
4 d
5 d

6 d
7 a
8 c
9 b
10 b

Chapter 4

PART 1

1 T
2 F
3 F
4 T
5 T

PART 2

1 d
2 b
3 c
4 a
5 c

6 b
7 d
8 d
9 a
10 a

Chapter 5

PART 1

1 F
2 T
3 T
4 F
5 T

PART 2

1 b
2 d
3 a
4 a
5 a

6 c
7 b
8 c
9 d
10 d

Chapter 6

PART 1

1 T
2 F
3 F
4 T
5 F

PART 2

1	d	6	b
2	c	7	a
3	b	8	b
4	c	9	c
5	a	10	a

Chapter 7

PART 1

1 F
2 T
3 T
4 T
5 F

PART 2

1	a	6	b
2	c	7	b
3	d	8	c
4	b	9	d
5	a	10	d

Chapter 8

PART 1

1 T
2 F
3 F
4 T
5 F

PART 2

1	d	6	c
2	b	7	d
3	a	8	a
4	c	9	b
5	c	10	a

Chapter 9

PART 1

1 T
2 T
3 T
4 F
5 F

PART 2

1	b	6	b
2	c	7	d
3	c	8	c
4	d	9	a
5	a	10	a